The Making of
MEMENTO

The Making of
MEMENTO

JAMES MOTTRAM

faber and faber

First published in 2002
by Faber and Faber Limited
3 Queen Square London WC1N 3AU

Published in the United States by Faber and Faber Inc.
an affiliate of Farrar, Straus and Giroux LLC, New York

Typeset by Faber and Faber Limited
Printed in the United States of America

Illustrations 1–13 © Newmarket Capital Group, by courtesy of Pathé
Illustrations 14–16 by courtesy of Daniel McFadden
Illustrations 17–18 by courtesy of Patti Podesta

James Mottram is hereby identified as author of this work in accordance with Section 77
of the Copyright, Designs and Patents Act 1988

A CIP record for this book
is available from the British Library

ISBN 0–571–21488–6

2 4 6 8 10 9 7 5 3

To Jerry,
Something to remember me by . . .

Contents

Acknowledgements

I would particularly like to thank all those who worked on *Memento* who gave up their time to talk about the film, namely, Chris Nolan, Emma Thomas, Jonah Nolan, Wally Pfister, Jennifer Todd, Aaron Ryder, Dody Dorn, Patti Podesta, Cindy Evans, David Julyan, Gary Gerlich, Bob Berney, Patrick Wachsberger, Guy Pearce, Carrie-Anne Moss, Joe Pantoliano, Mark Boone, Jr and Larry Holden.

I would also like to thank my editor, Walter Donohue, Richard Kelly, Marianne Gray, Michael Dillingham, Julie Keough, Tony and Debra McMahon and the staff of the BFI library and viewing facility.

Special thanks to: Swifty McBay, Ted Maul, Chris James and, of course, Tom 'What about this?' Lewis.

Visit: www.jamesmottram.co.uk

Introduction

Every one of us experiences a film differently but, for what it's worth, here's my *Memento*. One thing I guarantee is that it won't be yours. I've seen the film five times now; each time, it has caused a different emotional reaction. My first two viewings were in a small basement screening room in Wells St, London W1, in August and September 2000. The first time I saw it, appropriately enough I was with friend and former editor Jeremy Theobald, both the lead and co-producer of Christopher Nolan's debut, *Following*. I emerged bewildered and almost hollow inside, an empathetic emptiness for this man caught in a perpetual cycle of revenge. I was also confident I had a grasp on the mechanics of Nolan's intricate plot. My second screening left me dissatisfied: fully believing that, on going into the movie, I knew what was going to happen, I left the room frustrated, a feeling echoed by my companion that evening, who had seen the film for the first time. Bogged down with further questions about Leonard's back-story, a feeling of uncertainty crept over me; answers dangled tantalizingly, fading as dreams do, as my memory of the film diminished. Unlike the flourish of expositional information in the finale to *Following*, Nolan's second feature was beginning to prove much more elusive, a quality rarely achieved in contemporary cinema. Months later, with the knowledge that this book was in the offing, I watched the film on VHS for a third time. The feeling? Relief. The benefit of the 'pause' button allowed me to stop the film and think about what was unwinding before me, allowing me to re-assert my authority over the narrative. Twice more I watched it, either side of completing all the interviews for this book. The first of these caused me amusement more than anything, as my housemate guffawed her way through the movie, laughing at Leonard's wry comments about his condition. As you might expect, my most recent viewing, stimulated by hours of discussions with the film's key collaborators, evoked feelings of both enlightenment and obsession. But just in case you think I've found all the answers, I haven't. *Memento* is a film that rests and revels in ambiguity, the answers all there but necessarily obscured. I have settled, finally, for theories rather than answers. Like one of my favourite films over the past few years, David Lynch's *Lost Highway*, it concludes with a narrative loop – or in this case hairpin – that dares to return us, in some senses, to the beginning, exploding questions outwards like shards of flying glass. While I hope to answer some in the course of this book, I trust by the end you will still have some left.

James Mottram, September 2001

Memento

Above and opposite: Lenny (Guy Pearce) shoots Teddy (Joe Pantoliano), with gun and Polaroid camera.

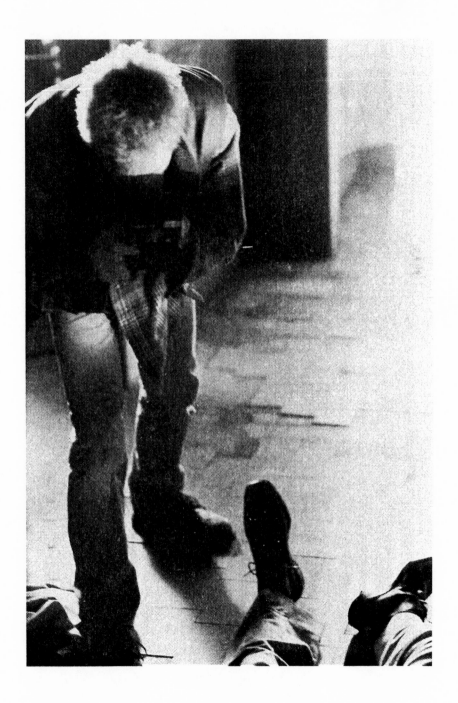

Lenny: 'What have I done?'

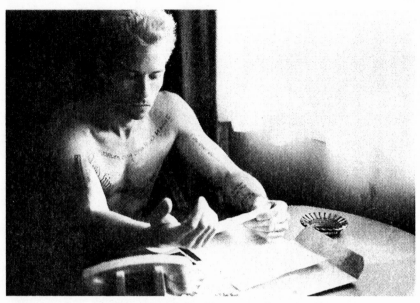

Written on the body; Lenny inscribes himself.

Lenny's murdered wife, Catherine Shelby (Jorja Fox).

Lenny meets Natalie (Carrie-Ann Moss) at the café – again.

Natalie tests Lenny's memory with a drink.

Lenny reads himself, under Natalie's watchful eye.

For Lenny and 'John G', the story comes full circle:
the end is the beginning.

Christopher Nolan and Guy Pearce.

Credits

CAST

Leonard GUY PEARCE
Natalie CARRIE-ANNE MOSS
Teddy JOE PANTOLIANO
Burt MARK BOONE, JUNIOR
Waiter RUSS FEGA
Catherine JORJA FOX
Sammy STEPHEN TOBOLOWSKY
Mrs Jankis HARRIET SANSOM HARRIS
Doctor THOMAS LENNON
Dodd CALLUM KEITH RENNIE
Blonde KIMBERLEY CAMPBELL
Tattooist MARIANNE MUELLERLEILE
Jimmy LARRY HOLDEN
Stand-ins CHAD LANE
SCOTT PIERCE
JENNY WORMAN

CREW

Writer/Director CHRIS NOLAN
Executive Producer AARON RYDER
Producers JENNIFER TODD
SUZANNE TODD
Director of Photography WALLY PFISTER
Production Designer PATTI PODESTA
Costume Designer CINDY EVANS
Music DAVID JULYAN

Line Producer ELAINE DYSINGER
Production Associate EMMA THOMAS

Unit Production Manager PAGE ROSENBERG-MARVIN
Production Supervisor BILL POVLETICH
1st Assistant Director CHRISTOPHER PAPPAS
2nd Assistant Director MICHELLE PAPPAS

Stunt Coordinator JULIUS LEFLORE
Stunts BRIAN AVERY
CHRIS DOYLE
COREY EUBANKS
STEVE HULIN
MONTE PERLIN

Post Production Supervisor JENIFER CHATFIELD
Post Production Consultant NANCY KIRHOFFER
First Assistant Editor MIKE GRANT

Camera Operator BOB HALL
First Assistant Camera PHIL SHANAHAN
Second Assistant Camera DANIEL C. MCFADDEN
Still Photographer DANNY ROTHENBERG

Set Decorator DANIELLE BERMAN
Assistant Art Director P. ERIK CARLSON

Property Master SEAN FALLON
Assistant Property Master TESSA 'LUCKY' CHASTEEN

Script Supervisor STEVEN R. GEHRKE

Production Coordinator LARRY T. LEWIS
Assistant Production Coordinator CHRISTINA KIM

Sound Mixer WILLIAM M. FIEGE
Boom Operator ACE WILLIAMS

Location Manager RUSS FEGA
Assistant Location Manager HOWIE SHERMAN

Key Make-Up Artist SCOTT EDDO
Key Hairstylist LARRY WAGGONER

Assistant Costume Designer LAURA MAROLAKOS
Set Costumer ANNE LAOPARADONCHAI

Special Effects Coordinator ANDREW SEBOK

Storyboard Artist MARK BRISTOL
Leadman DAVID MOCSARY
On-set Dresser MARILYN MORGAN
Swing Gang PATRICK BOLTON
WALSH CREEK CARVALHO
J. J. FLEISHER
Draftspersons ANDREW MAX CAHN
FANEE AARON
Art Department Assistants LIZ RUCKDESCHEL
JULIA D'AGOSTINO
JAY HADLEY

Gaffer CORY GERYAK
Best Boy Electric JIM MCCOMAS
Lamp Operators ERIC M. DAVIS
GREGORY E. MCEACHEN
DON SPIRO
RACHEL WELLS

Key Grip JASON NEWTON
Best Boy Grip DAVID BODIN
Dolly Grip KENNY DAVIS
Grips DAN LYNCH
R. MICHAEL STRINGER
LANDEN RUDDELL

Construction Coordinator PAUL A. STILL
Head Paint Foreman DAN DORFER
Set Painters RANDY BUDKA
JEFF LEAHY
DENNIS BIANCHI
Standby Painter LILLY FRANK
Standby Carpenter DEREK CHRISTENSEN
Propmakers LAMONT CARSON
WILLIAM F.GRAVES II
GABRIEL LOPEZ
CATHRYN SANNER
RUSS BROWN

Production Accountant WILLIAM POVLETICH
First Assistant Accountant DENISE MORA

13

Post Production Accountant ELIZABETH BERGMAN

2nd Second Assistant Director MICHAEL J. MUSTERIC
Assistants to Jennifer Todd ERIKA HEMMERLE
MARIANNE TITIRIGA
Assistants to Suzanne Todd MICHELLE GLASS
FRANK JOHNSON
Key Set Production Assistant MONICA M. KENYON
Production Assistants JONAH NOLAN
AUDREY TALLARD
CHARLIE YOOK
ED MCGRADY

Casting Assistant WENDY O'BRIEN
Extras Casting BILL DANCE CASTING
Casting Associate TERENCE HARRIS

Publicist AMANDA LAWRENCE

Transportation Coordinator P.GERALD KNIGHT
Transportation Captain JOSEPH R.FEENEY
Drivers ROBERT BLATCHFORD
BRUCE CALLAHAN
JOHN BUD CARDOS
GARY DEVOE
DAN DUFFY
DENISE FLIGG
CHARLES NEWLAND
SHAUN RYAN
STEVE 'SHOE' SHOEMAKER
KEVIN HALE SIMMONS
TRAVIS STAKE
DAN O.WISEMAN

First Aid ANTHONY WOODS
Construction Medic JANET BAXTER
Caterer CUISINE EXPRESS
Chef ANTONIO GARCIA
Helpers JOSE CARRILLO
RAFAEL HERNANDEZ
Craft Service RHONDA WHEELAN
CAJUN GUILBEAU

Newmarket Executives CINDY KIRVEN
BRENT AMELINGMEIER
DEBRA POLLACK
KENNETH KIM
RENE COGAN
JOHN CRYE
SCOTT LECLAU
LINDA HAWKINS

SECOND UNIT

First Assistant Director MARLON SMITH
Second Assistant Director ROBERT J. OHLANDT
Director of Photography JOAQUIN SEDILLO
First Assistant Camera DAVID J. HARDER
Second Assistant Camera RICH HUGHES
Key Grip KEVIN CHICKAUIS
Best Boy Grip SHANE TOULOUSE HOLLIDAY

POST PRODUCTION

Supervising Sound Editors GARY S. GERLICH
RICHARD LEGRAND, JR
Re-Recording Mixers MICHAEL CASPER
JONATHAN WALES
Recordist CHARLIE AJAR, JR

Music Supervisor DAVID KLOTZ

Music Editor MIKAEL SANDGREN
Sound Effects Editors WILLIAM HOOPER
PATRICK O'SULLIVAN
Assistant Sound Editor SAMUEL WEBB
Dialogue Editors WALTER SPENCER
NORVAL CRUTCHER III
Apprentice Editor CYBELE O'BRIEN
Post Production Assistant JAMIE BURRIS

Color Timers MATO DER AVANESSIAN
DON CAPOFERRI

ADR Supervisor NORVAL CRUTCHER III
ADR Mixers JEFF GOMILLION
ALAN HOLLY
ADR Recordist DIANA FLORES
Foley Mixer ALBERT ROMERO
Foley Artists DEAN MINNERLY
ROB MUCHNICKI
ADR Voice Casting BARBARA HARRIS

ADR Voices
TERRENCE BEASOR

VICKI DAVIS

JOHN DEMITA

JUDI DURAND

EFRAIN FIGUEROA

GREG FINLEY

JEFF FISCHER

DORIS HESS

RUTH ZALDUONDO

BOB NEILL

Negative Cutting MAGIC FILM & VIDEO

Titles and Opticals TITLE HOUSE
Post Production Sound Services provided by
UNIVERSAL STUDIOS SOUND
Digital Audio Loading provided by
DIGITAL DIFFERENCE

Additional ADR Services provided by
SOUNDFIRM. MELBOURNE

Grip & Electric Equipment provided by
THE LEONETTI COMPANY
Completion Bond provided by
FILM FINANCES, INC
Insurance provided by
AON/ALBERT G. RUBEN INSURANCE SERVICES INC

Production Legal Services provided by
STROOCK & STROOCK LAVAN
Additional Legal Services provided by
BENNETT J. FIDLOW

'SOMETHING IN THE AIR'
Written by David Bowie
and Reeves Gabrels
Performed by David Bowie
Courtesy of RZO Music.Inc./
Virgin Records America Inc.

'STONE'
Written and Performed by Monc
Courtesy of Conglomerated Industries

'GENERATION Z'
Written and Performed by Monc
Courtesy of Conglomerated Industries

'MOTHERLODE'
Written by Chuck Hamshaw
& Mark Schmidt
Published by JRM Music (ASCAP)
Courtesy of
Megatrax Production Music Inc. (1994)

'IPANEMA DREAMING'
Written by Daniel May
Performed by Daniel May
Published by Revision West (BMI)
Courtesy of Marc Ferrari
MasterSource

'DO THE BOOGALOO'
Written by Sammy Burdson
and Jean-Claude Madonne
Sonoton Music Library
Courtesy of Associated Production Music

SYNOPSIS

Memento is an inverted *noir*, a detective story told backwards in order to thrust the audience into the head of a protagonist who can't define himself in the present, but is forced to trust the conclusions of his former self. The subjective storytelling is intended to make us question familiar notions of revenge and identity.

Venice Film Festival catalogue, September 2000

The Making of
MEMENTO

Chapter 1

'It's beer o'clock. And I'm buying.'
The Critical Response

FADE IN:
INT. DERELICT HOUSE – DAY [COLOUR SEQUENCE]
A Polaroid photograph, clasped between finger and thumb, showing a crude, crime-scene flash picture of a man's body lying on a decaying wooden floor, a bloody mess where his head should be.

The image in the photo starts to fade as we superimpose titles. The hand holding the photo suddenly fans it in a rapid flapping motion, then holds it still. The image fades more, and again the picture is fanned.

As the titles end, the image fades to nothing. The hand holding the photo flaps it again, then places it at the front of a Polaroid camera.

The camera sucks the blank picture up, then the flash goes off.

As the Polaroid fades to white, so we begin with a blank slate . . .

It's the story of Leonard Shelby (Guy Pearce), a man who proves as emotionally empty as his surname suggests. Unable to make new memories since a blow to the head during a raid on his apartment, he remains hell-bent on avenging the death of his wife from that same assault. Hampered by his affliction, Leonard trawls the motels and bars of Southern California in an effort to gather evidence against the killer he believes is named John G. Tattooing scraps of information on his body, Leonard's faulty memory is abused by two others: bartender Natalie (Carrie-Anne Moss) and undercover cop Teddy (Joe Pantoliano), both involved in a lucrative drug deal.

It's also the story of how writer-director Christopher Nolan avoided the 'sophomore slump with flying colours', as *Variety* delicately termed it. No second-album syndrome here, for in *Memento* Nolan manages to significantly deepen the issues of identity and narrative pursued in his black-and-white 70-minute debut *Following*. The story of a would-be writer who becomes entangled in a murderous web of his own making after he meets a charismatic burglar who shows him the voyeuristic delights of his profession, its fractured time-line indicated just how willing Nolan was to challenge his audience. Raised in both the US and England, Nolan's mother is American, his father English, leading one critic to aptly call him 'a double-crosser himself'. He had been making Super 8 shorts (Action Man toys in science-fiction epics) with his father's camera since he was seven, collaborating with his brother and childhood friends Roko and Adrian Belic (who themselves would go on to make the award-winning documentary *Ghengis Blues*). All good prep in terms of fine-tuning his powers of resourcefulness, much needed on *Following*. Shot on weekends with friends from University College, London, where he studied English literature, it received a cursory UK release, after receiving finishing funds from Next Wave Films. With his third film – a re-make of Erik Skjoldbjærg's thriller *Insomnia* starring Al Pacino, Hilary Swank and Robin Williams – in the can, Nolan stands on the brink of widespread critical and commercial acclaim as he turns 30.

It's also a story of the resuscitation of film narrative. While twist-ending movies with unreliable narrators have been flourishing at the box office in recent times (*The Usual Suspects*, *Twelve Monkeys*, *The Sixth Sense* being the most memorable), *Memento* manages to out-manoeuvre them all. A modern *noir* about time, memory and identity, it delivers a sucker punch unlike any other. While *The Usual Suspects* closes as a mere shaggy-dog story and *The Sixth Sense* does no more than play paranormal games, *Memento*'s unique reverse structure lures us into a false sense of security; by the end, at the point we think we know absolute truth, Nolan whips the rug from right under our feet. What follows is an attempt to survey the reaction to *Memento* and introduce the reader to some of the theories and themes that surround the film.

The critics

I hope it's no shame to admit I couldn't understand *Memento*. Maybe I should have gone back and seen it a second time. Frankly, I couldn't face the exam it would set me . . . The feat of keeping so many bits of disparate and seemingly disordered information in one's mind was too much for me. Mensa champs might have accomplished it; I grew fatally confused, then resentful that such a brilliant idea should be so unnecessarily entangled in style.

Alexander Walker, *London Evening Standard*, 19 October 2000

One of the most honest reviews I have read for *Memento*, Walker's critique also lamented the fact that Nolan was not rewarded by his newspaper at their annual film awards for Most Promising Newcomer for *Following* – a film that led Walker to call Nolan 'an ingenious new talent who looks back to Stanley Kubrick's own polymorphous beginnings' – high praise indeed from a critic with strong personal links to the late Kubrick.

Likewise, Jonathan Romney began his review in the *New Statesman*:

I tend to take a lot of notes during press screenings; the more intriguing the film, the more notes. Sometimes I write so much that I miss entire chunks of the film. Then, when it comes to writing a review, I can't always read my own writing or remember exactly what a note means. So reviewing ends up being largely a process of deciphering my own notes and reconstructing in my mind the film that they supposedly refer to (but which I may already have half-forgotten). This probably means that my reviews are inaccurate and unreliable; but, if so, they are no more unreliable than anybody else's, or than memory itself.*

As you might imagine, Romney went on to draw comparisons with *Memento*, a film in which 'the hero is similarly confounded by his own note-taking'. Just as many of the more interesting critiques of the film showed, Walker and Romney found themselves unwittingly in Leonard's shoes; their task akin to his, they, unlike Leonard, were less prepared, their 'system' not as in tune as his. Unable to disconnect themselves from this world, they got a taste of what it was like to be Leonard Shelby.

Undoubtedly the best-reviewed film since *LA Confidential* three years before, it was clear from the outset that *Memento* would garner strong praise, surrounded as it was by a lacklustre selection of major-league films at the time (*Space Cowboys*, *What Lies Beneath* and the thematically related *Invisible Man* re-working, *The Hollow Man*, spring to mind). *Screen International*'s Lee Marshall, reporting from the Venice Film Festival, where the film received its first international

*Jonathan Romney, *New Statesman*, 23 October 2000

screening, immediately spotted the film's potential: 'That the ending leaves too many questions unanswered will, if anything, only boost the film's word-of-mouth appeal; *Memento* is the sort of film that gives rise to long post-screening discussions.' *Variety's* Lisa Nesselson, reporting from Deauville, where the film next played, called it 'a bravura tribute to the spirit of *Point Blank* and the importance of memory [that] deconstructs time with Einstein-caliber dexterity in the service of a delectably disturbing tale of revenge'.

The UK-based long-lead reviewers that followed were equally impressed. *Sight and Sound's* Chris Darke, for example, called it 'a remarkable psychological puzzle film, a crime conundrum that explores the narrative possibilities of *noir*'. *Empire*, meanwhile, called the film 'exciting, intriguing and exhausting . . . the promise Nolan showed with his no-budget *noir* debut *Following* has been borne out with an assured and original thriller'.

As can so often happen, sensational advance word can rankle some critics further down the line (*American Beauty*, for example, received a whipping from some national reviewers in the UK, fed up of being told it was the film of the year). 'Chris and I were real concerned that any minute there would be a backlash,' says *Memento's* Executive Producer, Aaron Ryder. 'The reviews were so good, it felt like somebody would take a shot at us. But it's just kept going. I saw a statistic that said we had 94 per cent good reviews.'

Indeed, the majority of the UK national critics, who saw the film before their US counterparts, were positive. Philip French, in the *Observer*, called it 'one of the year's most exciting pictures'; Anne Billson of the *Sunday Telegraph* noted it was 'a thriller that engages the brain from beginning to end . . . an intellectual roller-coaster'; Peter Bradshaw, in the *Guardian*, said that 'bobbing and weaving for 112 minutes, it is a film which somehow manages to keep you off balance and on your toes'. There were detractors, of course. Adam Mars-Jones in *The Times* said: 'Perhaps he's [Nolan] been influenced by Roeg's love of fracture, but the editing here isn't in the same class; memories of the assault are cut into the narrative with an aggressiveness that sometimes seems callow'; meanwhile, Nigel Andrews in the *Financial Times* added that Nolan 'weaves promising labyrinths for an hour. Unfortunately the film lasts two hours, by the close of which we are screaming for either enlightenment or release.'

By the time the US critics saw the film, *Memento* was already a cult classic. Elvis Mitchell, who would later conduct an enlightening interview with Nolan for the DVD, called the film an 'intense, through-the-looking-glass *noir*'. His colleague, A. Scott, noted that the film pulled off 'a dazzling feat of narrative sleight of hand'. Peter Travers, of *Rolling Stone*, called it a 'mesmerizing mind-bender . . . a mind-fuck as well as a new classic among thrillers'; Kenneth Turan, the *LA Times*' film critic, called it 'exceptional . . . a haunting, nervy thriller'; Joe Morgenstern, from the *Wall Street Journal*, said: 'I can't remember when a movie has seemed so clever, strangely affecting and slyly funny at the very same time.' Roger Ebert, in his *Chicago Sun Tribune* column, even batted away suggestions of plot holes (such as, How does the protagonist remember that he has short-term memory loss?) by saying: 'Leonard suffers from a condition brought on by a screenplay that finds it necessary, and it's unkind of us to inquire too deeply.'

The public
After the reviews, though, come the public. Glowing critical praise or not, *Memento* could still have suffered at the hands of the hardest audience to please – those who pay. Strong word-of-mouth was obviously vital. By December 2000, two months after the film had been released in France and the UK, it still had to make its US debut. The Internet buzz, by this point, was at fever pitch. 'Do yourself a favor, though, buy a ticket for the second show following so that your own short term memory doesn't forget the details,' said one web-head. The reaction on film-preview site Corona (www.corona.bc.ca) was typical, as reviews were being sent over from Europe. 'OK, now we really want to see this film and see if it's as good as all our UK readers say it is . . . Everything tells us so far that this is one of those films that flies in under the radar and surprises everyone.' That the film then flourished, as we shall see, in an unforgiving marketplace is testament to the fact that *Memento* is a movie that prompts coffee-shop debate. Chris Nolan's brother, Jonathan (known as Jonah), whose short story *Memento Mori* inspired the film, has a perspective typical of most:

> I got a phone call from a buddy of mine, who's a film studies student at Tisch Film School in New York. He called me up from a movie theatre, the Angelika in the Village in New York, having tried to get into a screening. This was the third weekend, and he had some

difficulty getting into the midnight screening. Then he watched two people get into a physical fight with each other, arguing about what the film was about. I can't remember hearing that about any other film. To be perfectly honest, I take a sick sense of pride being connected to something that has a power to do that. I don't expect people to sit around for the rest of their lives talking about it; it's just a piece of entertainment. I snuck out in New York and watched it with a group of people. I had read from chat-groups people saying, 'This is the first time I've ever seen total strangers stick around after the screening and talk about it with each other.' Sure enough, that's exactly what happened – and I'm tremendously proud of that.

As Jonah notes, chat-groups were put to good use where *Memento* was concerned. Too many to cover here, but the one I studied (www.cinephiles.net) contained what one would expect: healthy argument about the meaning of *Memento*. By way of introducing the myriad theories surrounding the film, here are some of the topics up for discussion. As I have already suggested in the Introduction, many of the film's plot points can only be speculated upon and Nolan himself is not about to put his cards on the table and reveal all. Here's what he has to say:

I believe the answers are all there in the film, but the terms of the storytelling deliberately prevent people from finding them. If you watch the film, and abandon your conventional desire for absolute truth – and the confirmation of absolute truth that most films provide you with – then you can find all the answers you're looking for. As far as I'm concerned, my view is very much in the film – the answers are all there for the attentive viewer, but the terms of the storytelling prevent me from being able to give the audience absolute confirmation. And that's the point.

The Insurance Scam. My personal favourite, one fan suggested that Leonard's wife faked her own death for insurance money. 'If not, why would she let Lenny continue to hunt for her killer?' Based on the confusing clip of Leonard in bed with his loved one, with the 'I've done it' tattoo on his chest, this person suggested it was a flash-forward to a time when they were re-united, with the wife masterminding the whole scam, even manipulating her husband.

The mental hospital. As reported by the film's website (www.otnemem .com) and the short story *Memento Mori*, Leonard has spent time in a mental institution. One particularly pedantic reader, after pointing out that Leonard would have crashed his car had he driven it, as he does, with his eyes closed for a few seconds in the film's close, added: 'I say he's still in the mental hospital and this is all in his mind.'

Remember Sammy Jankis. A popular one, given the fact that Teddy winds up by telling Leonard that Sammy was a con man, is that some think Leonard is Sammy (as evidenced by the three-tenths of a second shot of Leonard in the nursing home, in the scene where Sammy is committed). Or at least, he has distanced himself from his own past, and merged it with Sammy's story. With the brief clip of Leonard's wife, post the rape, under the plastic sheet but with an eye still open, it is suggested she may have lived. This could mean his wife had diabetes, despite Leonard claiming otherwise (it was possibly brought on after the attack, hence Leonard being unable to recall it). That Leonard is unable to make new memories would cover the fact that he accidentally killed her in the end by overdosing her with insulin – possibly goaded by his wife, in the way he remembers Sammy's spouse desperately trying to shake her husband from his memory loss. With the various shots of Leonard pinching his wife's thigh, along with the brief insert of a needle being flicked as Leonard notices his 'Remember Sammy Jankis' tattoo, Nolan does imply that this is possible. Returning to the 'I've done it' tattoo, it ties in to Teddy's suggestion that Leonard has already killed the real John G. As Joe Pantoliano theorizes: 'Leonard's wife is the one that tells him to start tattooing himself, in the hope that he remembers. That's why he's got that tattoo over his heart that says "I've done it".' But then why is there no sign of the tattoo now, or a scar where it once was? As some have suggested, Leonard's flashback to him lying in bed with his wife may just have been a figment of his imagination – an idealized fantasy of being reunited with his wife, and a convergence of memories – after the conversation he had with Natalie where he points out that the space round his heart is 'for when I've found him'. Leonard may well have been admitted into care after overdosing his wife, and then incited himself to escape and find his wife's 'killer' via his tattoos, having hooked up with Officer John 'Teddy' Gammell along the way. But as costume designer Cindy Evans points out: 'There is no solution. You'll never know how long he's been doing what he's doing, or how long he's been with Teddy being manipulated. You'll never know whether his wife is living or dead. You just have to let go of it.'

Suicide. As an alternative to this, while the wife may have survived the initial assault, she may have committed suicide (again, something Leonard would not remember), unable to take life without her Lenny. One web-user suggested that the police and the doctors have planted the idea in Leonard's head that he killed her, in an attempt to reveal the truth, by telling him '(with leading questions) that he killed her by giving her too many shots'.

The drug deal. This segment of the plot is more certain, as it happens across much of the film's two hours, but we are still left with questions. What is clear is that Natalie, who uses the bar where she works to set up drug deals for boyfriend Jimmy, sets Leonard up to deal with Dodd. Jimmy has disappeared (killed, of course, by Leonard, who then starts wearing his clothes and driving his Jag) with $200,000 in cash, owned by associates of Dodd's and Jimmy's, and Natalie senses she must protect herself by using Leonard. The deal itself was to be with bent cop Teddy. Beyond this, Jimmy and Natalie's connection to Teddy (and Dodd) is obscure: both refer to Leonard as 'the Memory Guy', indicating that Leonard has been mentioned by Teddy to them in the past. Jimmy, as he dies, also says under his breath: 'Remember Sammy', a fact that shocks Leonard into realizing he is being set up. As Teddy tells him, 'You tell everyone about Sammy' (undoubtedly true). Jimmy's last-gasp advice – along with his earlier disbelief after Leonard doubts that Jimmy may remember him – goes some way to indicate the depth of Shelby's involvement with him. However, why Jimmy requests Leonard to remember Sammy is obscure: perhaps in an effort to shake him from the murderous cycle he finds himself in.

One web-fan believes all are in cahoots with each other, but when Natalie meets Leonard (by accident); she uses him to her full advantage. Aware that Jimmy is dead (by Leonard's vehicle, his apparel and the coaster he has with her handwriting on it), she then sets him up to remove Dodd and then Teddy (even pointing Leonard towards the same derelict building he killed Jimmy in, showing she was well informed about the initial drug deal). The reader even theorizes that Teddy and Natalie may have initially been in on the deal together, hence the lack of surprise on Teddy's face when he finds a bound-and-gagged

Dodd in the wardrobe. This is unlikely, given that Teddy tells Leonard not to trust Natalie, though by this point he may be scrambling to save his life, aware that she may be using Leonard to turn on him. What is not clear in the film is what happened to Natalie; the last we see of her is in the restaurant, handing over the photocopy of Teddy's licence-plate, knowing full well Teddy will soon be dead. As she says, she and Leonard are 'survivors', so one thing can be sure: she's still alive at the end (or rather the beginning) of the film.

As Carrie-Anne Moss told *Cinefantastique*:

Natalie's trying to save her own life. Her reactions to what is happening are motivated by her need to survive. In one scene, Natalie is throwing out the garbage behind her bar when she thinks she sees her boyfriend Jimmy pull up in his car. She takes a look in the car and sees that it is not her boyfriend but Leonard. She reacts with a mild 'Oops, sorry. Wrong person.' Now, another woman, one who wasn't as streetwise as Natalie might have reacted with suspicion or fear or anger. Natalie lives in her own world, a world of *I'll stab you, you stab me – anyone can be fucking you over at any time*. And so when she sees that the man in the car is not Jimmy, she doesn't know what's going on, so she's piecing it all together, like: 'What's happening here? Who is this person?' A million things are going through her mind at that point, and then she goes away, and she's trying to figure everything out. I think Natalie is used to being in situations like this, but I'm sure she's been involved in worse things, where she's had to pretend everything's okay, then had to find her way through it, to make sure she gets out all right. I always think, like in my own life, with somebody bad you maybe act nonchalant, so you can get out of it.*

As for Teddy, the question hangs over his head: Has he been using Leonard as a patsy, a terminator with no moral conscience? Fighting for his life (an important point, given what he says), Teddy tells Leonard: 'You don't know who you are . . . let me take you down to the basement and show you what you've become.' Is there a basement full of rotting victims, or is Teddy just buying some time? In relation to the theory that Leonard and Sammy's histories overlap, as one viewer noted, 'in Leonard's case the doctor was Teddy and the electrified objects were the

* *Cinefantastique*, April 2001

murders that Teddy was tricking Leonard into repeating over and over'. How long have they been together? If we are to believe Teddy, at least a year, as he shows us the picture of Leonard pointing to himself, after having reputedly despatched the real John G. Why then does Leonard not, by the end of the film, need to take a Polaroid of Teddy? Surely he should already be in possession of one. My guess is that it was Teddy who only recently gave him the camera as a way of helping his 'system' of remembering things. We know that Teddy snapped a picture of Leonard a year before, and it remains in keeping with the idea that Teddy, while crooked, genuinely likes Leonard. Joe Pantoliano is sympathetic towards his character. 'I think that it wasn't Teddy's intention to get Jimmy killed. As he says to Leonard, "What the fuck did you do?" Everything changes in this instance. He takes his identity, puts on his clothes, is driving his car. This is not the way it was meant to be.'

That said, who then is on the phone in the black-and-white segments talking to Leonard, pointing him towards the latest John G.? We assume Teddy, and certainly it must be at the beginning of the black-and-white scene that leads Leonard to the derelict hallway to encounter Jimmy. Mark Boone, Jr, who plays motel clerk Burt, would disagree, though.

'You can't assume it's Teddy. It doesn't really make sense, in what Leonard is saying, for Teddy to be having this conversation. I found that part of the movie only to be expositional. This is why I haven't spent much time thinking about it, because I don't see that it logically, validly pieces together.'

Perhaps Teddy was not expecting Leonard to succeed. More likely, he was not aware that Leonard would snag the man's clothes and car. Teddy does spend much of the film attempting to get Leonard out of town, partly to save his own life, and partly because he knows people will start asking questions if they see Leonard kitted out as Jimmy, potentially leading the trail back to Teddy. At one point, just after Leonard has killed Jimmy, Teddy intercepts him at the tattoo parlour, where he clocks the fact that his own licence-plate number is being burnt into Leonard's leg. Banking on Leonard having no recollection of the recent murder of Jimmy, Teddy – who, depending on the situation, has a habit of disguising his true identity from Leonard – claims to be a snitch, who is in contact with a cop looking for Jimmy. The cop, he says, has been calling him, slipping letters under his door, feeding him 'a line of crap about John G. being some local drug dealer'. This is exactly what we assume Teddy to have just been doing; but things have changed. Teddy needs Leonard out of town – though, in keeping with a constant motive of his, he first needs Leonard's car. As evidenced by the goggle-eyed expression on his face when Leonard opens the trunk of the Jaguar, Teddy wants the $200,000 stashed inside.

As Joe Pantoliano says: 'The big through-line for Teddy is to get that money out of the car. Chris explained that to me. I asked him, "Well, why don't I just steal the fucking car? The guy goes to bed doesn't he? I'm a cop! Why don't I just steal the car?" He said it's because Teddy likes Leonard.' Certainly Teddy, from the outset, has been trying to trick Leonard into handing him over the keys to the Jag, without drawing attention to his crime.

His 'condition'. This is where a number of people split. How does Leonard, if his attack is the last thing he recalls, remember he has a memory problem? One theory, as mentioned by Joe Pantoliano, is that Lenny's wife organized the early tattoos – with the 'Remember Sammy Jankis' statement there to remind Leonard of Jankis's story, and hence his own memory loss. Through conditioning, he now knows that he has this problem. What is clear is that Leonard knows the pros and cons of his predicament; he knows he can deceive himself into killing Teddy, and have no memory of it afterwards. He also knows how to circumvent the limitations of his affliction, as shown by the way he hires the blonde escort to plant his wife's things around him. As Nolan himself has said:

> That was a scene I was always prepared to defend, because I always assumed that someone would try to make me cut it out, because . . .
> it doesn't necessarily relate that much to the story. To me, it's the first moment in the film that we're given a strong indication that Leonard understands how to manipulate himself. Essentially, it provides a small model of what the entire film comes to represent, which is that on some level he is aware of the fact that he can . . . 'communicate with his future self', because he doesn't have the connection of memory between the two selves.*

Some have been unable to accept that Leonard would be able to repeatedly incite himself to avenge his wife. One viewer points out that if Leonard's condition is really just like waking up every ten minutes or so, then surely he must be constantly in a state of grief, and yet he is

*Creative Screenwriting, March/April 2001

able to 'recite with total certainty what the medical diagnosis is in his case and what the police attitude to his statement and handling of his investigation would be'. Another noted:

> He must indeed be spending all his awake hours reading through the Cliff Notes of the case (and losing all the information every fifteen minutes) to even have the faintest clue what he is doing. The habit and conditioning story wouldn't work to explain his uncanny ability to know what's in his own notebook, and case-map, because learning a host of different causal/semantic relationships (this clue indicates this, this piece of evidence goes there) is a far cry from learning not to pick up cylindrical blocks by aversive conditioning.

In Nolan's defence, Leonard does say, at one point: 'I've got a copy of the police report. It has lots of information, but with my condition, it's tough. I can't really keep it all in mind at once.' Beyond this, all I do is grant Nolan some dramatic licence, in allowing his character's mind to function in the way it does. Of course, the fact that Leonard's 'condition' does not fully play out as it should do, opens up a further avenue: Is Leonard faking?

One fan points out that every time there is a knock at the door, Leonard quickly decides to cover his tattoos up. 'This implies that he is aware of them and wants to hide them, which implies that he has more memory than he lets on.' As another example, the chase with Dodd starts with Leonard trying to calculate where he is, and who is chasing whom. 'He can't remember fleeing his own car as Dodd shoots out the window, yet he does have the mental recall to go straight to the Jaguar without consulting his pictures.' It could be argued that both of these actions come from conditioning, but equally maybe Leonard's memory has partially returned; perhaps he did kill his own wife and can recall this but, for safety's sake, has projected his actions onto that of Sammy, and wants to absolve himself by catching the man involved in her initial rape. Certainly, Leonard's unflappable facade – given the fact that he spends much of his existence disorientated – would suggest he, like Sammy Jankis, knows how to fake everyone out. Even himself.

Memento and the presence of time
Undoubtedly one of the most intricately structured films ever devised, *Memento*'s talking point – a film that runs backwards – is highly deceptive. The obvious comparisons are to Harold Pinter's play

Betrayal and Martin Amis's novel *Time's Arrow*. In the former, a story of adultery between friends, the narrative works its way back from the break-up of a relationship through disenchantment, complications, happiness and finally to innocence. Pinter's work turned on the irony that the characters grew happier as the play progressed, while the audience was all too aware of how the story would pan out. In Amis's story, a first-person account from death back to the birth of a Nazi, the reader is fed a bewildered commentary by the protagonist as he reviews his life as if in reverse. Leading to the point in the concentration camps when he witnesses dogs 'mending' prisoners' faces, the atrocities of the Holocaust are given a frighteningly naive slant. Nolan had read *Time's Arrow* years before, but wasn't even aware of the Pinter play. Either way, his motives for using a backwards-stepping narrative were entirely different. Unlike Amis, Nolan is not interested in social commentary, or re-viewing history through fresh eyes. Pinter, meanwhile, plays on granting the audience knowledge over his characters, with the break-up of the relationship that opens the play remaining the most important 'event' in our minds. All the action that follows (and leads up to the divorce) is presented to comment upon that opening scene. Nolan, though, leaves us (almost) as confused as Leonard. The death of Teddy, as we move backwards, ceases to become as important as Leonard's own journey.

In many ways, comparison between these three works – written for very different mediums (although Pinter's play was turned into a film in 1983) – is spurious, given that *Memento* does not truly carry a backwards structure. Nolan thinks it's helpful for people to think of it in this way, to understand the film, but he prefers a different structural model. 'If you draw out the time-line, it is indeed a hairpin. If you order the material chronologically, the black-and-white material moves forwards, and in the last scene switches around and goes backwards to the colour scene. So there is this hairpin turn.'

Breaking this idea down, this is how the film concludes. The final backwards-moving colour segment of the film begins with Leonard's screech to a halt outside the tattoo parlour (where he will significantly request Teddy's licence-plate number to be inscribed on his leg, setting him on a journey that will ultimately lead to Teddy's death – as seen at the film's outset). When the scene closes, Nolan takes us back to the black-and-white sequence where Leonard leaves the motel, meets Teddy, and heads to the derelict hallway, chronologically just before

33

the tattoo parlour scene. As Leonard later takes a Polaroid of the dead Jimmy Grantz, the film fades into colour, as the Polaroid develops, at one of the film's most elegant but understated moments. Leonard, unsettled by Teddy's revelations in the derelict hallway, decides to choose him as the next John G., copying his licence plate down, knowing he will soon forget his murderous intent. The next step? The tattoo parlour, of course, and the skid to a halt.

Time is no longer a universal constant, running in two different directions and, after a small jink, meeting in the middle. As one critic noted, 'Think of a watch whose minute hand revolves clockwise and whose hour hand revolves counterclockwise.' 'You can never find out where you are in the time-line, because there is no time-line,' says Jonah Nolan. 'If it was a straight-backwards film, you could just take that two-dimensional time-line and flip it over, but you can't do that with this film. Later on down the line, you realize that this film doesn't run back; it's a Möbius strip.'

The geometric shape that half-twists back on itself, looping around to finish where it started, is most fitting for a plot that one critic called 'effectively one continuous twist from start to finish'. Such a structure has been most successfully deployed in David Lynch's 1997 film *Lost Highway*. A film even more complex than *Memento*, it was one Chris Nolan enjoyed immensely. 'To me, it worked on the level of a dream. I enjoyed it much more afterwards than I did watching it. But I do feel it's an impenetrable film in narrative terms. In terms of telling the story of that film – and there is a story – I could not personally get it; I could not get those specifics. With *Memento* those specifics are there, they're just incredibly hard to put together and incredibly hard to find.'

Unlike Bill Pullman's Fred Madison in Lynch's film – who arrives outside his own front door to whisper a message he himself heard at the beginning of the film – Nolan plays no such tricks with Leonard Shelby. 'Leonard is not in a backwards world. He doesn't see his story as backwards. He's just in the moment,' he says. For Leonard himself, time is moving forward, rather than looping back on itself. Nolan points out the film's narrative structure, rather than a true Möbius strip (though he confesses his brother's analogy is apt) is a cycle in an ever-widening gyre – in other words, a spiral of chaos that Leonard is perpetually sliding down.

In many ways, you could also think of the film's two time-lines as being pulled together, folding in on each other and imploding. Props and physical characteristics are Nolan's favoured devices to pull the two segments together, 'clues to the objective chronology', as Nolan puts it. For example, the paper bag in the black-and-white sequences that has 'Shave Thigh' on it is discovered by Leonard after Burt (in a colour scene) takes him, accidentally, to his former room; Leonard's scratches are also absent in these black-and-white scenes, suggesting again that these moments occur before the colour sequences.

Nolan also uses a number of verbal and visual devices right from the beginning to ensure we can tune in to the chronology of events. Aside, obviously, from the credit-sequence murder of Teddy, whereby the scene literally winds backwards, Nolan deliberately makes the first reverse-shifts memorable. Our first clue is the Polaroid of Teddy with 'Kill Him' written on it, which Leonard consults just before he kills him. Two colour scenes later, where Leonard is preparing to leave his motel to find Teddy, we see him writing this very startling command on the photo. In the same scene, Nolan stages a discussion between Leonard and motel clerk Burt that crystallizes the experience the audience are about to undergo. Leonard describes his condition as 'like you always just woke up'; as we shall see, at the beginning of each colour segment – roughly the length of Leonard's short-term memory span – Leonard begins disorientated, and so will we. As Burt replies, 'That must suck. All . . . backwards. Well, like . . . you gotta pretty good idea of what you're gonna do next, but no idea what you just did.' It's a beautifully understated expression of the structure. 'I wanted to have a bit early on where they basically did explain what the audience was going to go through,' says Nolan. 'I think there's a limitation as to how much the audience can take on of the specifics of that, but it does suggest this disorientation.' At the very end of this scene we are treated to the second sight of Teddy, with his grating cry of 'Lenny!' By this point, this line already memorably delivered at the beginning of the previous scene, it's becoming clear that we are moving backwards. As if to emphasize the point, Nolan pans the camera right to left as Teddy enters the door. Later on, Nolan enjoys a joke as he gets Leonard to say to his wife in a flashback: 'the pleasure of a book is in wanting to know what happens next'. He knows very well this 'pleasure' has been substituted for us by the urge to find out what went before.

Across the time-line of the film, though, time is compressed with elliptical shifts. As production designer Patti Podesta points out: 'There are slow-downs in the time, as we move backwards. It's not just that everything moves at the same amount of time, and we're marching backwards.' For example, Nolan uses jump cuts in the sequence where Leonard has just tied up Dodd, as he sits down on the bed. The segment where Dodd is run out of town also crosses from day to night. Within the scenes there are also cycles of time; while relaxing at Natalie's house, we see Leonard flip through his Polaroids before the film cuts to later in the day, where, still on the couch watching TV, he sees his Sammy Jankis tattoo and automatically begins to flip through his photos once again. A crafty moment, it highlights the perpetual process of loss and recollection he goes through.

Nolan also uses repetitions a great deal, partly – as he says – to 'show how the same situation can be viewed very differently, depending on what information you already know up to that point'. As an example, think of where he's searching for a pen (hidden by Natalie, of course). Natalie comes in with a bruised face, and Leonard is sympathetic to her plight; later, we see what led up to this. Natalie berating Leonard, then merely going outside while he forgets her barrage of insults about his wife. The 'Remember Sammy Jankis' tattoo also plays very differently, from the first (in the motel) to the last (in the car, just before the skid-to-a-halt) time we see it. By the end, we begin to suspect Leonard is not thinking of Sammy to recall the fundamental differences between their tales. 'Great story,' says Teddy. 'Gets better every time you tell it. So you lie to yourself to be happy. Nothing wrong with that – we all do. Who cares if there's a few little things you'd rather not remember?' Leonard also repeats that he never said Sammy was lying; the first time he says it, his tone is full of guilt for what happened. When he later implores, 'I *never* said he was faking! I never said that,' his voice is more defensive, as he tries to rebuff Teddy's revelations. The early reference to the Gideon Bible being one of the few items to be found in an empty motel room is also later repeated by Leonard, when he opens a drawer in Dodd's apartment. As he spies the gun on top of the Bible, he stops mid-sentence, hinting at how much deeper he is now involved than when he last uttered those words.

Ask Nolan about how he sees these repetitions fitting in, and the response is frank: 'Well, that's where it gets complicated. It's true of the action, and also of the story elements. There are direct repetitions and then there are echoes, if you like, or indirect repetitions. It's an outward spiral, a widening gyre. That's true of the back-story: where do you think this piece of the story we're showing you over two hours fits? But it's also true of scenes within that two-hour cycle – wheels within wheels.'

Nolan also dislocates the narrative to such a degree that even certain lines of dialogue are reacted to long before the feed-line has been delivered. Burt, for example, announcing to Leonard: 'You said you like to look people in the eye when you talk to them.' Much later, in a black-and-white segment, Leonard explains this to Burt down the phone. As Nolan says of novelist Graham Swift and *Waterland* – his fractured Fens-set story of three generations and another structural influence on Chris – 'He has an incredible structural approach to time-lines, clueing you into what's going on so much that by the end of the book he's leaving sentences half-finished and you know where they're going.' It's an affect Nolan achieves with the script to *Memento*.

The futility of revenge and the *film noir* tradition
'Thirty-three years ago, after making his cinematic debut with a small-scale black-and-white movie in Britain, John Boorman went to the States and became a world figure overnight, directing Lee Marvin in *Point Blank*, a very European treatment of an archetypal American subject. The 29-year-old Christopher Nolan has done something similar.'*

Christopher Nolan had never, so he says, seen John Boorman's *Point Blank* before or during the making of *Memento*. Given the uncanny parallels – a revenge *noir* set in California that, as French says, 'repays with interest its debts to Alain Resnais' – it's a rather surprising fact. 'I can certainly understand the parallels,' admits Nolan. 'It's very similar in the way it starts, throwing you into this chronological turmoil. Also, the revenge motif, it's taken to such an extreme. I'm never surprised to see other films people have made that have done the same kind of things as me; we're all working in the same realm, and we're all drawing from everyday life, and books and experiences.'

Boorman's 1967 film opens with Marvin's Walker – double-crossed by his pal and girlfriend – wounded, close to death, as he lies in an empty cell of the deserted Alcatraz prison. As the recollections of a dying man flood back, the words 'a dream, a dream' fill the screen. The titles roll (looking uncannily like a film's closing credits), as we see ghostly, frozen stills of the protagonist scaling the wire fence of Alcatraz, while

* Philip French, *Observer*, 22 October 2000

the voice of a tour guide explains that escape from the prison is virtually impossible. That we then see a smart, healthy Walker begin his quest for revenge and the pursuit of the $93,000, which by rights is his, we assume this man achieved what few ever have, his flight from the island driven on by sheer will. As his vengeful journey takes him through various tiers of the crime organization he attempts to penetrate, his progress goes strangely unhindered. Trawling through a near-hallucinogenic landscape, Walker's search is what becomes important; as David Thomson has said, Walker is 'a man for whom the game has suddenly become more valuable than any prize'.* Concluding with an enigmatic riddle that leaves us wondering whether what has preceded is merely a delirious revenge fantasy, the last-gasp triumph of a man on his way out, *Point Blank*, as Thomson suggested, 'may be still the richest merging of an American genre with European art-house aspirations'.

It would be fair to say that *Memento*, whether influenced or not by *Point Blank*, is very much in the same tradition, Nolan unwittingly taking the baton from Boorman. Think of Leonard's quiet, unassuming memories of his wife around the house, devoid of sound. Likewise, Walker's rose-tinted rain-washed recollections of his stroll along the San Francisco waterfront with his loved one are soundless, only Johnny Mandel's swooning theme to be heard. Kindred artistic spirits, Nolan and Boorman understand too the futility of revenge.

As Natalie tells Leonard: 'Even if you get your revenge, you won't remember it. You won't even know it's happened.' Leonard's snappy reply is a desperate moment of self-defence. 'The world doesn't disappear when you close your eyes, does it? My actions still have meaning, even if I can't remember them. My wife deserves vengeance, and it doesn't make a difference whether I know about it.' As he later (or earlier) explains to Teddy, in an echo of this conversation, he's living just for revenge: 'That's what keeps me going. It's all I have.'

In a time when Hollywood seems content to foist nasty-minded efforts like *Payback* and *8mm* onto us, films that have no regard for the consequences of revenge, Nolan is one film-maker attempting to redress the balance. 'It seems to me that too often, in films, things that should be disturbing aren't, but are used for short-term, superficial narrative advantage. I was interested in reclaiming the concept of revenge, and hopefully making the audience look at it in a different

*David Thomson, *Sight and Sound*, June 1998

way from other movies, where the revenge element is simply an excuse to view the main character going off and killing someone.'

An emotion strong enough to sustain Walker's wild fantasies (whether imagined or not), revenge becomes Leonard's life-blood, the idea of retribution more central to his life than the act of vengeance itself. Unable, as Natalie points out and Teddy later proves, to remember his acts of vengeance, Leonard becomes locked into this ever-widening gyre, as Nolan would say. A cycle of destruction that has yet to satiate his desire for revenge, it's a cruel trick of his condition that keeps him there. 'I want time to pass,' he says. 'How can I heal if I can't feel time?' As Nolan says, 'That moment [the rape] is totally separate from present day. Leonard can't get a handle on the difference between those two time periods. He doesn't know if it's six months or two years.' Leonard's transformation from avenging angel to surrogate psychopath is a timeless one, his moral conscience subdued – and manipulated – by the loss of his short-term memory. Revenge becomes a concept more than an act; unable to remember it, Leonard's dilemma prompts the question of whether the act can exist, in any real sense, outside of one's own head. Does it have any value beyond personal satisfaction? – a point that *Point Blank* surely also raises. Yet Leonard sustains his anger throughout, through the very fact that he has been rendered, in a manner of speaking, impotent. 'He took away the woman I love and he took away my memory. He destroyed everything; my life and my ability to live.' In a curiously asexual *film noir* where even a call-girl leaves the scene untouched, Leonard's potency has been replaced by a longing for a (seemingly) dead woman. As Jonah Nolan says:

> It's what Teddy says at the end of the film; he's the hero of his own romantic quest. I wanted Chris to have Teddy say at the end – which Chris ultimately rejected and in hindsight was right to do so – 'You loved your wife, but how much more did you love your dead wife? How much easier is it to love your dead wife?' Having her taken away is much easier; now she's preserved in aspic, as it says in the short story. Locked away in a filing cabinet, she becomes a memory, not a person.

Memento is very much a distillation of *film noir*, stripping down the parameters of the genre to their purest possible form, using its trappings to subvert. The film's narrative recalls a familiar generic pattern: the chief protagonist, a lone figure on the periphery. Certainly, the motels, Ferdy's bar, the derelict house are typical settings we associate with *film noir*. The characters – undercover cops, dealers, prostitutes and so on – are also familiar, as is the theme of betrayal and revenge; every character – from Burt (the first person we realize is using Leonard) to Sammy ('a con man', says Teddy), and including Leonard – is lying to another or himself. Paranoia – the feeling of not knowing whom one can trust – also comes into play. Yet examining these customary tropes via the prism of Leonard's extreme situation causes a refraction. Like the film's colour scheme – blue rather than black, cream rather than white – everything has been painted afresh. As Nolan has said:

> I felt that we had a situation here that would allow us to freshen up and re-awaken some of the neuroses behind the familiar elements. You know, the betrayal, the double-cross, the *femme fatale* – all these things function very powerfully in the way they were intended in the old *film noir* by exaggerating our fears and insecurities. I felt that by taking this particular approach and filtering it through this concept, we would be able to re-awaken some of the confusion and uncertainty and ambiguity that those types of character reversals used to have, but lost because we've come to expect those kinds of surprises.*

Take Natalie, *Memento*'s so-called *femme fatale*. Despite her cool ice-blue eyes, Moss is no Lauren Bacall, and rather than sizzle with sexual energy, her line readings are deliberately without any hint of a come-on. Natalie, more blue-collar worker than rich bitch-on-heat, uses her cunning – rather than her sex – as her weapon. Despite the indication that she and Leonard may have had sex when the scene opens in her bedroom, the film is chaste enough not to show any intercourse (closing with Leonard slipping into bed, the previous colour sequence began with the pair waking up, coyly avoiding any such revelations). While we are unable to tell if Natalie is genuinely aggrieved to have lost Jimmy, or is just manipulating her emotions to fool Leonard into saving her neck, the photograph she shows him goes some way to indicate the love she had for her boyfriend. Leonard, of course, becomes the image-double of Jimmy, dressed in his clothes and a surrogate 'lover' for a woman who 'has lost someone'. Like Teddy,

---

* *Creative Screenwriting*, March/April 2001

Natalie, while using Leonard, has feelings for him. As Carrie-Anne Moss says:

> I feel even that with the times she is manipulating Leonard, she does really care about him, and the fact that a woman cares about a man and he doesn't remember because he has this [memory] condition, it's sort of a major rejection . . . She lets Leonard walk by, and then she grabs him, and is like, *Okay, he's just not going to remember me.* She says to him in the scene before – which is the scene after that in the movie – she kisses him and says, 'Don't you remember me?' He says, 'No' and she says, 'I think you will.' And then he hadn't. So she thinks, 'Ah, this one's not going to work.'*

More emotionally ambiguous than what we might expect from a *film noir*, what does this make *Memento*? As J. Hoberman noted in his review: 'The video stores are filled with examples of retro-*noir* and neo-*noir*, but Christopher Nolan's audacious timebender is something else. Call it meta-*noir*.' A postmodern fable filmed in the information age, *Memento*'s hero is a renegade gumshoe, an amateur private eye strangely (yet aptly) dependent on handwritten notes and fading Polaroids – the latter flashed like a detective's badge; both a symbol of his quest and an assured definition of self. The distinct lack of electronic paraphernalia – bugs, camcorders, tape-players, computers, cell-phones – indicates just how out of step Leonard is. Just as the tattoo reads 'Never Answer The Phone', so Leonard is marooned from modern technology. Unable to learn how any piece of equipment fresh to him would work, he is left with a bulky (and incomplete) file that he must, as he puts it, 'summarize' to understand. As Teddy says: 'You don't know who you *are*, who you've become since the incident. You're wandering around, playing detective . . . and you don't even know how long ago it was.' With his 'freaky tattoos' and his incomplete file of information, Leonard is a walking text, his life and his mission literally carried at all times on his person.

To complete the circle, *Memento* also has much in common with the superlative *Double Indemnity*, Billy Wilder and Raymond Chandler's archetypal adaptation of James M. Cain's novel. Like *Memento* and *Point Blank*, *Double Indemnity* begins at the end as Walter Neff (Fred McMurray) staggers, seemingly shot, into the office of a colleague to flick on a tape recorder and tell his tale, the story of how he, an insurance agent, connives with the glamorous wife (Barbara Stanwyck) of a client to kill her husband. Like Leonard, Barton Keyes (Edward G. Robinson) is an insurance claims investigator, who shares many of Shelby's analytic skills. A film that influenced a generation of *noirs* with its retrospective narration, we always know what Neff's fate will be, whatever he says or does. *Memento*, of course, leaves us less certain, but Nolan's deliberate nod to the world of Wilder's film goes some way to show how he wishes to revitalize the 'nostalgic image of guys in raincoats and fedoras coming down alleyways', as he puts it.

Unlike *Double Indemnity*, *Memento*'s voice-over begins, and predominantly remains, in the second-person – immediately dislocating Leonard from himself. 'So, where are you? You're in a motel room,' he says. During these black-and-white 'confessional' sequences, Leonard exists in the sanctity of the one space where he can achieve some form of stability. Outside, for Leonard, all is chaos – but inside the room, he is master of all the facts. Such a 'confessional' state recalls Wilder's film – the Neff flashbacks are structured to achieve a retrospective examination of his current moral/criminal state. Yet *Memento* also employs another form of 'investigative' flashback. A common currency in *film noir*, it sets out to re-examine past events to solve a recent crime. *Memento*, of course, turns it on its head – beginning with the resolution to the murder, and retracing its path, undermining us every step of the way. In *Memento* a very modern *noir*, even betrayal and revenge are acts stripped of their certainties.

Memory and the question of identity

How is it that we know who we are? We might wake up in the night, disorientated, and wonder where we are. We may have forgotten where the window or the door is, or the bathroom, or who's sleeping beside us. We may think, perhaps, that we have lived through what we just dreamed of, or we may wonder if we are now still dreaming. But we never wonder who we are. However confused we might be about every other particular of our existence, we always know is this: That we are now who we have always been. We never wake up and think, 'Who am I?' because our knowledge of who we are is mediated by what the doctors of the mind call our self-schemata, the richest, most stable and most complex memory structures we have. They are the structures that connect us to our past, and allow us to connect to our futures. To lose those connections would be a sign of pathology, a pathology called 'amnesia'.

The above quotation could quite easily be mistaken for a description of *Memento*. With reference to the uncertainty of waking up, it feels like the nightmarish existence that is Leonard's life. As it states, our sense of self ensures we never question who we are – unless we suffer from amnesia. In fact, this is the opening monologue to David Siegel and Scott McGehee's audacious but overlooked 1993 meta-*noir*, *Suture*. Meaning either medical stitching or a term of Lacanian theory concerning the relationship of the individual subject to its place within language, the word 'suture' makes for an intriguing title, as the film deals with both definitions.

The tale of two half-brothers, Vincent Towers (Michael Harris) and Clay Arlington (Dennis Haysbert), the story begins after the latter is nearly killed by a car-bomb, planted by his relation. Under suspicion for murder of his father, Vincent had already hidden his own ID on Clay, before lending him the vehicle. Hoping to evade the murder rap by faking his own death, his plans go awry when Clay survives, albeit needing extensive surgery to his face. When he comes to, Clay is now mistaken for Vincent – and, now suffering from amnesia, is unable to argue otherwise. While Clay replaces Vincent as chief suspect, what remains fascinating in the film is that Dennis Haysbert himself is black. His skin colour is not acknowledged by anyone; shot in black-and-white Scope, Haysbert is the only black actor to be seen in the film. It's as if we've landed in a world literally drained of colour.

Co-directors McGehee and Siegel have stated they wanted to construct a story around the issue of identity, rather than make a film commenting on the black experience in America. As they told Jonathan Romney: 'We've attempted to keep the film more in the parameters of sociology than of race, the way the homogeneity of society affects the construction of personal identity.'* With Leonard's identity as anonymous as the culture around him, one could argue that Nolan makes a similar point. Also like *Memento* (see Chapter 6), the film makes great use of mirrors to prompt the question – as the above monologue notes – 'How it is that we know who we are?'. The

*Sight and Sound, February 1995

43

fact that a mirror is used to outwardly confirm to ourselves that we are who we think we are is suggested by Siegel and McGehee marvellously – most notably, as Clay removes his bandages and first checks his face. The camera catches a reflection of Dr Renée Descartes (Mel Harris), the female surgeon responsible for re-constructing Clay's face, suggesting he has been created in an image that came from her. Set in the symmetrical city of Phoenix (its main-street axis echoed by the Rorschach blot on the office wall), it's a film of reflections – and like *Memento*, what is shown in the glass does not always tell the whole story.

As if to emphasize the kinship between the films, they also set about visually deconstructing *film noir*. While Nolan shades his film in inky blues, so Siegel and McGehee deliver a white-and-black *noir*, partly suggesting the clinical feel that runs through the film. Nolan calls *Suture* 'a cool film', adding that he met both film-makers at the Sundance festival, where their second feature, *The Deep End*, played alongside Nolan's sophomore effort. 'They came to see *Memento*,' he says. 'Afterwards, I was talking to David Siegel, and he said, "Yeah, it was quite in the realm of *Suture*." You can definitely see the connections.'

Amnesia in films is not a new subject. Most famously, Alfred Hitchcock's Dalí-influenced 1945 film *Spellbound* (a direct influence on *Suture*, with its murder plot) told the story of a paranoid amnesiac (Gregory Peck) posing as the new head of Green Manors mental asylum. *Memento*, though, bears little comparison to Hitchcock's work – given that Leonard knows who he was, not who he now is. A more fruitful contrast is with the aforementioned *Lost Highway*. At the halfway point in Lynch's story, co-written with Barry Gifford, sax player Fred Madison is arrested and imprisoned for murdering his wife; after a hellish interlude, Madison transmogrifies, it would seem, into garage mechanic Pete Dayton (Balthazar Getty). Described (not, initially, by Lynch, but by the film unit's publicist Debra Wuliger) as 'a psychogenic fugue', it's the perfect metaphorical description for both Madison's journey and the film itself. A form of amnesia, which is a flight from reality, the word 'fugue' itself is a musical term that describes a theme that starts, which then is taken up by a second theme, with the first continually supplying a counter-theme. Indeed, as Dayton's story plays out, the spectre of Madison haunts the plot, until he returns in the final reel. Absolved, it would seem, of his inner demons – via the telling of Dayton's story – Madison is able to recover his soul and return from the fugue. Interestingly, both *Memento* and *Lost Highway* position their protagonists as potential wife-killers – hinting that this most extreme form of self-deception (amnesia) is a physical manifestation of the guilt they feel.

While *Lost Highway* was dubbed a '21st century horror-*noir*', it could hardly be called science fiction. Yet the genre, in recent cinema history, has seen two key films – both inspired by books from author Phillip K. Dick – deal with the question of memory. Ridley Scott's 1982 effort *Blade Runner* and Paul Verhoeven's *Total Recall* eight years later both asked: 'Are we our memories?'. The latter – from Dick's *We Can Remember It For You Wholesale* – dealt with notions of memory-implants, ultimately posing the conundrum: 'If you can insert false past experiences, is what you are now witnessing any more real?' Like *Blade Runner*, with its androids known as Replicants, memory becomes the 'self-schemata' we cling to as a way of defining who we are in relation to the world. Take that away, and we have no history in the world, no interaction with it, and therefore are left stranded. Faces in the crowd become just that – and we have no way of distinguishing if those around us have any relevance to our lives.

Minus any new memories, Leonard's own sense of self, however, is malleable. We see him, across the film, in three different guises. As Leonard the insurance investigator, he is logical and methodical, convinced that Sammy is faking. This is, of course, a flashback – or even a distortion. In the black-and-white sequences, when Leonard is telling this story, he is in his second personality phase – more trusting and honest, as he reflects upon the possibility that he is being manipulated. Finally, in the colour scenes, Leonard is at his most deceptive. A hero looking to avenge his wife, he is both chivalrous (helping Natalie) and savage (killing both Jimmy and Teddy). He is a man able to change his identity almost at will.

Likewise, the issue of identity is at the core of John Frankenheimer's 1966 film *Seconds*, a film that relates to both *Suture* – with its use of plastic surgery as a means to change identity – and to Nolan's own films. 'I loved the film and thought about it a lot in relation to *Following*,' says Nolan. 'Not in terms of subject matter, but the style. It's beautifully shot by James Wong Howe, with the hand-held camera. Very, very unusual. I think I took on board a certain amount of that for aspects of *Memento* as well.' Indeed, Frankenheimer's opening sequences – where the camera and actor are both mounted on the dolly, providing an uncomfortably close close-up – resemble Nolan's thinking, as the camera virtually hangs off Leonard's shoulder, to show his point of view. But *Seconds* has more in comparison with *Memento* than Nolan might think. The story of tired-of-life businessman Arthur Hamilton (John Randolph), who gets a chance to 'disappear' and start a new life, via a covert organization, it sees the protagonist undergo facial reconstruction, before being shipped off to live the American Dream in LA. Given the life and face of artist Tony Wilson (now played by Rock Hudson), our hero then realizes that the dream of freedom is just that. He's no better off a new man. As much an attack on materialism as anything, it is ultimately a film about moral responsibility. Like Leonard, free of moral constraint because of his amnesia, Hamilton – once he emerges as Wilson – is told he is now 'absolved of all responsibility, except of your own interest . . . You don't have to prove anything anymore. You are accepted. You will be in your own new dimension'. While his actions are less deadly than Leonard's, he has similarly ducked out of society and, to some extent, its rules.

Seconds, like *Memento* and *Suture*, bases itself on a situation that is more metaphorical than realistic. Yet while some have questioned the accuracy of *Memento*'s depiction of anterograde amnesia, or short-term memory loss, it would seem that Nolan – while not planning for a medically accurate rendering of the condition – has given Leonard's affliction a lot of thought. As a cognitive psychologist who wrote in to the Internet discussion board featured above pointed out: 'Leonard could remember whatever he's thinking about indefinitely, as long as he is intent upon it. However, the slamming of a car door, for instance, could distract him for a moment, and then a long train of thought would derail.' AA, he goes on to explain, is 'not so much an inability to record new memories but to be consciously aware of them'. He cites the story of a patient with AA who shook hands with his new doctor, who had a pin concealed in his palm. The next time they met, the patient had no recollection of the doctor, but would not shake hands with him. Leonard, too, has this sensation through the film; at one point, after his fight with Natalie, we see him rubbing his fist, aware that he has hit something, but unsure what it was. His subsequent expression borders on distrust when he talks to Natalie. Likewise, the shell-cases he discovers in Teddy's pick-up truck by the derelict house in the film's opening were dropped there earlier by him (seen at the end of the film, after he sits in the driver's seat and notes down Teddy's number plate). Again, his quizzical expression when he re-discovers the shells indicates he is subconsciously aware of the fact that he put them there.

Nolan's film also questions the fallibility of memory. Teddy, in the diner, tells Leonard his notes may be unreliable. His reply is thus:

> Memory's not perfect. It's not even that good. Ask the police; eye-witness testimony is unreliable. The cops don't catch a killer by sitting around remembering stuff. They collect facts, make notes, draw conclusions. Facts, not memories: that's how you investigate. I know, it's what I used to do. Memory can change the shape of a room or the colour of a car. It's an interpretation, not a record. Memories can be changed or distorted and they're irrelevant if you have facts.

In many ways the key speech of the film, it contains the very crux of Nolan's argument and Leonard's experience. His own recollections are subject to change, as we will see when he deliberately writes down Teddy's licence-plate number, knowing he will forget that he has falsified this evidence. As Guy Pearce says, Leonard 'operates almost like a synapse really, just a nerve ending that's responding to everything around him and trying to maintain some sort of control'.

Of course, this should be amended, as Leonard is very much a disconnected synapse, a man emotionally stranded from his experience who, as Mark Boone, Jr notes, ends up in 'a place of utter, desolate loneliness . . . a very lonely and desperate man looking for a connection'. As we know, the word *memento*, Latin for 'remember', means a reminder of the past, something that can trigger a memory. One of the most poignant scenes in Nolan's film is the shot of Leonard at the refinery burning his wife's things, his remaining mementoes of a life he once had with her. He murmurs: 'Probably tried this before. Probably burned truckloads of your stuff. Can't remember to forget you.' It's a devastating line that encapsulates his dilemma. His feelings permanently on hold, his last memory – he believes – is of his wife dying. Forever grief-stricken, his faulty memory is unable to accumulate new experience as part of the healing process.

One can argue that his memory is a tool he manipulates to reconstruct his uncertain past in a way that confirms a 'truth' more loyal to his needs than the facts themselves. Driven by a desire for revenge, yet forever adrift in the present, Leonard must remember the past in a way that not only continually motivates him towards his goal but simultaneously banishes from his mind his own culpability for his past. As Teddy says 'I guess I can only make you believe the things you want to be true, huh?'

As we began this chapter with two accounts of critics confounded by their own limitations of memory, it seems fitting we should end with *Memento*'s lead actor – who began to think about the issue of memory in relation to the task of learning to play Leonard:

> As soon as I read the script, I had a bit of a chuckle about it, because I'm always questioning my own memory anyway. And not because I would consider it to be bad, but because of the different ways your memory is broken up. People are continually saying to me: 'Gee, you're an actor, you must have a good memory. How do you remember the lines?' It seems to be a common misconception that actors must have great memories. I have real paranoia about my memory and I don't know if it's because my mother keeps telling me my father had a real photographic memory and I wonder if I'm angst-ridden that I should live up to that. Since doing the film it's made me question it even more. Particularly in relation to things like my father. My father died when I was very young and I'm always asked about my memory of him. I really have no idea as to whether I remember him, or whether I just have created this memory of him via the stories my mother has told me and the photographs that I know.

Chapter 2

'I have to believe in the world outside my own mind.'
Releasing *Memento*

The US release

On 24 March 2000, the unthinkable happened: *Memento* was passed over. The Friday before Oscar weekend, three screenings were arranged in Los Angeles for distributors. *Memento*'s producers, Jennifer and Suzanne Todd, the sister team that makes up production company Team Todd, attended one each, Executive Producer Aaron Ryder the third. 'Everyone was so hyped to see the film. People had read the script, so they knew what it was going to be. The film is the best version of the script, obviously. Everyone was trying to bully us into seeing the film first, so we did all these screenings on the Friday night,' recalls Jennifer Todd. Every single studio head was there; Todd sat next to her former boss, Miramax head Harvey Weinstein. 'I'd worked for him ten years ago, as an executive. He passed [on the film] to my face; he just said, "Oh, it's not for us. He's a talented film-maker, and we should try and find something to do together, but it's not for us,"' remembers Jennifer. It was the same story with every other major distributor:

> It was horrible. I could not get drunk fast enough. Having to tell Chris was so awful. He doesn't care so much; he's the guy who could make movies in his basement alone, and he'd be fine. It phased him a bit, but I think it hit Aaron and I much harder. We come from the world of 2000 screens. We were so proud of the film, and we thought it was so cool. The friends we had shown it to were our smarty-pants friends – intelligent, film-savvy people. They had responded so well to it. I couldn't imagine that distributors were not responding in the same way.

Left with the sound of 'I don't know if people will get it', or 'It's hard to stay with', ringing in her ears, Todd met with Ryder afterwards at the Four Seasons Hotel to drown their sorrows. 'It was one of the worst weekends of my life,' reflects Ryder now. Banking on an edgy company like Artisan Entertainment (who boldly orchestrated *The Blair Witch*

Project's release) biting the bullet, he, like the Todds, could not quite comprehend what had just happened. 'These were very dark days,' he says, bluntly. 'All the distributors felt it would be hard to market, and it was too small. Some of them found the film frustrating, I think. Maybe it just wasn't right for them at that time.'

Chris, on the other hand, was typically stoic in his acceptance of the film's rebuttal:

> I kind of expected it. I always expected it to have a hard time getting it out there in its purest form. I always thought there would be this moment where I would be asked to start compromising. Luckily that was not the case. But I always knew this was a film that distributors weren't necessarily going to get. I wasn't seeing very exciting things coming out of the independent distributors anyway. I had spent a lot of time showing people the script, who worked in those types of companies. The reactions had been very varied. People were interested in it, and in the craft of it, and in what I was doing next, but not in the script itself. So I was used to the levels of rejection that the project could have. To people who loved it, who helped make it, that was baffling. But it didn't really surprise me that much.

Joe Pantoliano remembers not being surprised at the studios passing. The following night, he was – as was Chris and his then-girlfriend-now-wife Emma Thomas – in attendance at the Independent Spirit Awards, there to present an award. His experience that night was typical. First on the list of studio personnel to accost him, armed with praise, was Artisan Entertainment President Bill Block:

> He comes over and says, 'Joey, it's such a good movie. You're incredible in it!' I said, 'Oh, thank you. You gonna buy it?' He said, 'No.' Then, later on, Russell Schwartz, who was at Gramercy, came across the room and said, 'Joey Pants, Joey Pants! *Memento* – what a picture! It's a killer.' I said, 'Thanks, Russell, you gonna buy it?' . . . . 'No'. The next night at the *Vanity Fair* party, Harvey Weinstein – who I'd never formally met – sees me from across the room and says, 'Joey Pants? *Memento* – what a great film. You're fucking great in it.' I said, 'Thank you, Harvey! You gonna buy it?' . . . 'No.' Poor Chris Nolan; they put all their eggs in one fucking basket. Everyone was in town; if Harvey had said he wanted to buy it, then everyone wants to buy it. It was in limbo.

Only Tri-Mark Pictures, which had previously released such 'difficult' films as Catherine Breillat's explicit *Romance*, stepped forward, showing any interest. 'We were dead set against that,' says Jennifer Todd. 'They weren't bad, they were nice people. But they were much smaller than we envisaged.' Within a couple of weeks, representatives from Paramount Classics came back saying they would like to release it, but after a couple of meetings, the 'low-ball offer', as Todd puts it, made to Newmarket was rejected. Pantoliano recalls a frantic Ruth Vitale, Co-President of Paramount Classics, confronting him later on at the SAG awards. 'She said, "Joey, you've been telling everybody that nobody wanted this movie. That's not true! I wanted to buy this movie! I loved this movie!" To her credit, she was one of the few that wanted to buy it – but for five cents. She shorted them!'

Chris Nolan concedes that the Todds and Ryder were thinking in business terms when rejecting the offers made, but he felt, at least partially, validated that some distributors had shown genuine interest. 'While it wasn't embraced by those who would put the most money in, the film – at every stage – had its advocates. To me it was most important that the company that bought it loved the film. That said, there's definitely a sense that if somebody isn't willing to pay a decent sum of money for the film, how much can they really love it?"

With the film left in limbo, Chris and Emma found themselves in a familiar position. Just as distributors had largely dismissed *Following* because it was black-and-white and under feature length, so they rejected *Memento* owing to its reverse structure. 'That was a really tough time for us,' says Emma, who co-produced *Following* and was associate producer on *Memento*. 'It was quite bizarre to then show it to distributors – who all, by the way, said they loved it but just didn't have faith that they could make any money from it. Ultimately, that's what it comes down to.'

It was a thought that horrified Steven Soderbergh, the man whose debut film *sex, lies and videotape* almost single-handedly re-invigorated the US independent cinema movement a decade before. Currently on a roll, following the success of both *Traffic* and *Erin Brockovich*, Soderbergh – now more of a father-figure for aspiring low-budget film-makers – made his feelings patently clear during interviews. His remarks to website *FilmThreat* were typical: 'I saw a film under circumstances that, to me, signalled the death of the independent movement. Because I knew before I saw the film that everyone in town had seen it and declined to distribute it, which was Chris Nolan's *Memento* . . . I watched it and came out of there thinking "That's it. When a movie this good can't get released, then, it's over."'*

As Nolan recalls: 'He happened to be recommending it just before he became the most successful movie director in the universe. The timing was wonderful for us.' Impressed by Nolan's evident talent, Soderbergh – along with his *Out of Sight* star George Clooney – went on to executive-produce *Insomnia*, recommending Nolan for the job of director. 'He became a champion of the film around town, helping create the buzz about it,' says Jennifer Todd. 'As a film-maker, I think he was devastated that there was this great young film-maker, who'd made a cool film, and no one would release it. He did his bit as a heavyweight, going around complaining and being very vocal in interviews about it.'

Nolan was finally able to meet the director, in connection with the *Insomnia* project; he found, in him, a kindred spirit. 'I was able to thank him for talking up *Memento*; he didn't really have a lot of questions to ask. He'd seen the film the same way I had. He'd seen it and responded to it. You get fewer questions from people who really tap into the film in the way I viewed it. The questions are less important than the thing itself. He told me he'd seen *Following* in London, which I thought was pretty impressive considering the short time it played there.'

Nolan had deliberately avoided catching Soderbergh's own film *The Limey*, which was released while *Memento* was in production. 'People had told me it had a similar unconventional approach to chronology, and I wanted to not have anything in my head that was similar.' But during their meeting, after Nolan had finally seen it, the discussion inevitably turned towards the film. 'Steven felt we'd done similar things, in terms of taking a formerly mainstream genre and applying a more experimental approach,' remembers Nolan.

Another California-set revenge drama that deconstructed time, it starred Terence Stamp as a career criminal hell-bent on avenging the death of his daughter, who he suspects was involved with Peter Fonda's laid-back record producer. 'Tell them I'm coming!' bellows Stamp after a bruising; moments later he's on his feet and gunning his assailants down. Like Leonard, and Lee Marvin before him in *Point Blank*, he is relentless in his task. What remains distinct in the film,

* *Filmthreat.com*, 25 March 2001

aside from Stamp's explosive performance, is the fractured narrative that Soderbergh twists the story around. Opening with Stamp in a taxi cab leaving LAX, within minutes the film runs us ragged through time, as we lurch into past recollections of his girl, spliced with fantasy-projections, clips of him back on the plane and ahead in his lonely hotel room. Quietly orchestrated by Soderbergh, it's a technique used to highlight the protagonist's volatile mental state. 'Seeing *The Limey*, what it does with time and structure is incredibly different from *Memento*,' Nolan reflects.

The common misconception around Hollywood, though, was that Soderbergh had secured *Memento* a distributor. 'It was very ironic,' says Todd. 'I ran into a girl in Sundance who was in the film business – I won't name names – but didn't know I was one of the producers on *Memento*. She said, "Oh, y'know, I helped that movie get distribution. I told Soderbergh to see the movie, and then he found it a distributor."'

While his influence obviously didn't hurt the film's reputation, by the time Soderbergh saw the film, a distribution and festival strategy was already in place. Undoubtedly a brave step, Newmarket chiefs Will Tyrer and Chris Ball decided to release the film themselves. 'I got an inkling before other people,' says Nolan. 'It was very clear to me that Will really loved the film. He'd seen it several times. Chris Ball similarly. I felt from that an attachment to the film that was bound to mean that they wanted to find the best way of getting the film out there. It kind of made sense to me, and I felt it was a great compliment to the film, that they didn't feel they could just give it away to somebody else.'

To this point, Newmarket had only fully funded one film, *Cruel Intentions*, though its investments – in films like Jim Jarmusch's *Dead Man* – underlined its commitment to risky projects. Distribution, however, of a film passed over by the studios was another matter entirely. 'This was a company whose faith in this film had never shaken,' says Ryder, who was initially responsible for introducing Nolan's script of *Memento* to Newmarket. 'These are the two guys, when everyone passed on it, who had the balls to say: "We're gonna do this ourselves." A lot of other companies I could think of would've sold it to HBO or put it straight out on video.'

Their decision was a relief to Patrick Wachsberger, President/CEO of Summit Entertainment, who frequently handle Newmarket projects in the international market. Summit had been with *Memento* since the beginning. 'I loved the movie from the get-go, so I was totally shocked when no one bought it. You get to the point where you think, "Maybe it's time to leave the business. Maybe I don't get it anymore."' A company with a history of working on prestige independent films (*Bound*, *The Blair Witch Project*, *Sleepy Hollow*), Summit's job was to hawk Nolan's screenplay across the world, pre-selling the distribution rights and simultaneously securing contributions towards the film's budget. While foreign sales were not dependent on a US release, Summit and Wachsberger still held a financial and emotional stake in the film.

So much so, that Wachsberger had himself disagreed about the date chosen to screen the film to the US market, feeling most potential buyers would be distracted with thoughts of winning golden statues that weekend. 'I had a big argument at the time with Will Tyrer, at Newmarket, about the date chosen to screen the movie to the domestic distributors. I said it was the wrong time, the wrong date, and was not the way to do it. I said they should wait about two weeks. They decided to do it anyway, and it was a big fiasco. Some distributors didn't stay to the end of the screening; their minds were elsewhere. I bumped into a lot of distributors that night, and it was pretty discouraging.'

In retrospect, says Wachsberger, they all got lucky. Having met Chris Ball and Will Tyrer back when he was involved with Ridley Scott's Christopher Columbus yarn *1492: Conquest of Paradise*, he was still surprised that they decided to distribute the film domestically. 'It's pride of ownership, I guess. They have a larger share of the movie than we do. Will and Chris had set up a video business, which was very lucrative, and said, "We are going to need to distribute films domestically, because we're buying some titles for video where the film-maker really wants a theatrical release, so why don't we start with a movie we all love – *Memento*?" To which we said, "Why not?" They didn't have much to lose.'

What it did mean was that *Memento* did not have to be test-screened, a fact that relieved Jennifer Todd:

That is the worst part of making a film. The studios make you go and do these test screenings, where you have to listen to 300 people dragged off the street critique your film. It's horrible. Most of the time, you do it in LA, and half of the people are struggling film-makers themselves, and they bitch about the *mise-en-scène* in your movie! And you just wanna kill yourself! We never had to do that on *Memento*. Other than showing it to friends, and watching the movie internally, the first time any of us saw it with an audience was at the Venice Film Festival. Which was great. I loved that.'

The first step was to bring in Bob Berney, a veteran distributor who, coincidentally, had just begun working for new US independent distributor, IFC, a company that a few years before had funded Chris Nolan's *Following*. A former theatre exhibitor himself, Berney was initially just asked to come in and view the film. 'At the time, I didn't know anything about it. I didn't know if it had or had not gotten any offers. I just came in cold to see the movie. I was alone in a screening room. I was blown away by it; I was further amazed to hear that they were having any kind of problem whatsoever finding a home for the film. I had an amazing gut instinct. Not only was this director a find, but so was the cast. I don't think the distributors really thought it through.'

Berney already had experience in releasing titles left in limbo: the previous year, October films had found themselves unable to distribute Todd Solondz's *Happiness* after a ruling from their parent company Universal, who balked at the film's taboo subject matter. Berney was brought on by the film's producers, Good Machine, to form an ad hoc one-off distribution company to release the film. Taking $3.8 million, the film did respectable business, given that, as Berney says, 'it did not cross over beyond the art-house and to the 'burbs'.

'The Newmarket guys were curious,' recalls Berney:

Could this be done? Can a producer really do their own distribution? My answer was 'Absolutely!' I had just done it on *Happiness*, even though it was a one-time situation. I had told them, 'If you're willing to put up the money to back up what you want to do . . .' I mean, it's one thing to want to do it, but you also have to be prepared to take the financial risk. They believed in the film enough not to give up in any way. I told them that as long as they put up the proper amount to match a fairly aggressive release, and just let me do it, I thought we could really make it work. I wasn't going to predict that it would do as well as it did, but I knew it would work.' (He predicted a gross of around $5 million at the time.)

Money for p&a (prints and advertising) had to be found, to cover advertising, publicity, creative materials, and even the cost of shipping prints. 'Most independent producers couldn't really do that, and it's risky,' says Berney. 'Because I was able to assemble a team that had had experience doing that, they felt confident – and they believed in the film too.' Creating a distribution company from what he calls 'smoke and mirrors', Berney set about planning the marketing and release strategy, with the rare luxury of having *carte blanche* to plan the film's launch.

'I was really comfortable working with Newmarket. It was kind of rare. They'd say, "We're financiers and producers, not distributors. So we're gonna go with you." Luckily it worked, because it was all put on me to make these decisions because they didn't have that experience. They went with it, and it worked in the end.'

Initially, the feeling was to launch the film in the US in the fall at the New York Film Festival, which would act as a curtain-raiser for an October release. 'We kind of thought it might be invited to the New York Film Festival,' says Berney. 'Ultimately, it didn't work out, and we were going to have to make a really brutal decision. If we'd rushed it, we would not have had the success we've had.' Without that autumnal platform to launch from, it left *Memento* jostling for screens in a packed Oscar-friendly holiday season. 'Bob was scrambling to see what theatres we could get, but we were scared that if we went too late we would be boshed by the Christmas movies,' remembers Todd.

It was decided, instead, to wait for Sundance in January 2001, returning Chris to Park City, where *Following* had played (as part of the simultaneous Slamdance Film Festival) two years previously, before settling on a 16 March opening date, almost a year to the day after the film was roundly rejected by the major studios. 'I wanted to wait until March, really to have the luxury of time,' says Berney:

> To let the Internet campaign grow, to let the trailer play out. I think the launch through the web campaign was really a factor in the film's success. It's hard enough for the big studios at Christmas time. They're overspending all sorts of dollars at that time, and it is very tough to come in then, and let the film sit there at the theatres. We were able to really have plenty of screens. It was doing so well, that it was able to hang in there. There wasn't the pressure that Christmas brings [in March].

Much of Berney's job was completed before Christmas. With the film set to travel the foreign festival circuit (see below), Berney had already spent time at the Toronto festival negotiating sales with exhibitors, as well as working on advance publicity. 'Bob has a great relationship with theatre owners,' says Ryder:

That ultimately can make or break you: the ability to get your movie into theatres, and keep it there. That's the biggest hurdle to accomplish. He came up very early on and said, 'If we're going to do this right, we have to let the audience discover the film. We build a platform release.' In other words, you release it on eleven screens in New York and LA, and that's it. A week later you go to seven cities, and then the week after that you go further. It's truly a ramping up, platform release. While it was tempting, when we were hitting high numbers in New York and LA, to try to blow it out on 500 screens immediately, we would've not had the success we had.

When the film opened in the US on 16 March, in New York and LA, it followed Berney's recommended pattern. Opening in certain key theatres, such as the Lincoln Plaza, on New York's Upper West Side, the downtown Angelika Theatre and Loews 19th St theatre, both near NYU, *Memento* was given the chance to reach a wide audience. 'We had an interesting mix of theatres giving the potential of a cross-over right away,' said Berney. 'Through NYU, we really reached a younger crowd. We tried to cover the demographics.' Similarly, in Los Angeles, the equivalent of the Angelika, Laemmle's Sunset 5, was booked, alongside more commercial runs in the Valley. 'We took a bit of a gamble, going for the art house and the more suburban commercial run,' says Berney.

Opening against Steven Seagal's comeback *Exit Wounds*, Jean-Jacques Arnaud's Stalingrad Siege flop *Enemy at the Gates* as well as low-key movies *Gabriela* and *American Desi*, it was a dream week to make your bow. The following week saw lightweight vehicles like *Heartbreakers* and *Say It Isn't So* released, again not encroaching upon *Memento*'s core audience. Only *Amores Perros*, another rave-reviewed effort, which opened on 30 March, could be seen as touting for the same kind of film-goer. 'There was nothing in the genre around the same time,' says Berney. 'There were some quick action films, and some comedies, so I think we benefited from an abundance of formulaic fare. That's one reason we really stayed around. We certainly were completely different.'

Week two saw a small rise to fifteen screens, before the number hit seventy-six in its third week, with the film making its bow in Dallas, Washington DC, Boston, Seattle and Philadelphia. '*Memento* absolutely worked across the board in every city,' says Berney. 'It played very strongly in the key upscale theatres, but also playing very deep into the suburban runs, that maybe play independent films only every now and again. It played the big circuits. It really did get into the culture.'

By this point, Miramax's Harvey Weinstein had realized his mistake. Rumours circulated that Miramax, some four weeks into *Memento*'s US run, wanted to buy the film from Newmarket. It would mean an extensive Oscar campaign for the film, as well as money spent on maintaining the number of screens the film was showing on. Jennifer Todd remains unsure whether that would've happened. 'Harvey was very sincere in the fact that he screwed up and didn't pick up the film. There was talk that Miramax wanted to buy the movie and then do a release for it. I don't know if that was coming from agents or Harvey himself. Whether or not it came from Harvey or the agents, I know for a fact that Newmarket weren't interested in that.' Indeed, having suffered the indignity of being passed over, why should Newmarket buckle a month into the film's run? Now, it was merely a case of managing the film's countrywide release.

'Bob's point was that if you just throw this out there, without the right amount of publicity, without doing your homework and letting the word of mouth trickle down, it's never going to work,' says Ryder. Spending four weeks in the top ten, and sixteen weeks in the top twenty, during a summer that saw the release of such box-office juggernauts as *Pearl Harbor* and *Shrek*, the strategy clearly worked. With screen averages reaching as much as $9,705 a week when the film was playing on a handful of screens, it was clear the film's reputation was spreading. The film reached eighth position in its eleventh week, having grossed $2,395,290 in that seven-day period at the end of May. The same week also saw the film hit the highest number of screens it would play on, at 531.

'When we got into release, it became about managing the success and adding the theatres in, hopefully, a smart way,' says Berney. 'The real trick is to be restrained. You don't want to expand it too quick, and go crazy. You're better off trying to wait, and let the word-of-mouth build, because it takes a while to get out to the rest of the country. Even though it's a media frenzy in New York and LA, it takes four to six weeks before you can have that advance awareness in, say, Dallas or Chicago. We could have gone higher, but we really tried to keep it at a good level that we thought the film would perform at.'

By late September, at the time of writing, the film is still playing in just under one hundred theatres across the country, with a cumulative box-office total of $25,481,198. 'I really think the distributors thought American audiences wouldn't want to stay with a slow-moving, unravelling mystery thriller,' says Todd. 'They thought it was too smart for them. The great punctuation to the whole story is that they were wrong. The movie spread so much wider than we thought it would. The fact that the movie has made $25 million so far is crazy.'

As Berney points out, with the film surpassing various 'lofty' milestones (the $10 and $20 million marks), the ancillary value for video and pay television has increased rapidly:

> There's so many independent films that never make $1 million. Most of them don't. It's very tough to ever get there. I was surprised at the level it finally achieved. I wasn't surprised that it played there, because of the genre elements and the cast. The fact that it fools the audience . . . studio movies like *The Sixth Sense* have proved that they will go and see films with twists and turns. What I was just surprised at was the sustaining power, that it kept going and people saw it over and over again.

So successful has *Memento* been, the film was released on DVD in the US on 4 September 2001, while still playing in the cinemas there. 'The reason it came out was that we did our deal early on, not knowing the film would still be in theatres in August,' says Aaron Ryder. Extras included a tattoo gallery, showing stills of Leonard's body-art, trailers for both *Memento* and *Following*, Jonah Nolan's short story *Memento Mori* and a 25-minute interview with Chris Nolan. Understandably, no audio commentary was provided by the director, given his desire to keep the secrets of the film under wraps. In the DVD was an 'Easter egg' leading to the rumoured re-ordering of the scenes, enabling the viewer to watch the film in chronological order. 'The movie's meant to be shown this way [backwards],' explains Ryder, less than impressed at the idea. 'The idea is that you're putting the audience at a disadvantage of learning information; to try to put it back in order . . . it's a gimmick, in a way, but you're undermining the intent.' A film that benefits repeat viewings, its sell-through shelf-life looks secure. As Ryder says: 'I think

Memento is going to be one of those films, like *Blade Runner* or *The Matrix*, that will be around for a long, long time.'

Foreign markets and the festival circuit

Let's take a step back, though. Prior to the film's US release, *Memento* had already successfully opened in France, with distributors UGC, and the UK, with Pathé. 'Ironically, the film always had foreign distribution, even when it didn't have American distribution,' recalls Jennifer Todd. 'Because Summit were involved, they were always partnered with Newmarket, and so when we were locked into the European festivals, they went and built a release pattern around that.'

Summit Entertainment had been involved after Aaron Ryder first brought Patrick Wachsberger the script. '*Memento* was not a movie when it came to us,' says Wachsberger. 'It was a screenplay, with a young director attached. Chris had done *Following*, and Aaron was pushing for *Memento* to really become a movie. I really liked the screenplay, and we decided to do the movie together. We became the insurance, so to speak.'

Despite the potential of the script, personnel in Summit were split over whether to jump on board:

> Some people – who will remain nameless – just didn't get it. They felt it was complicated, and at the end, it doesn't really deliver. I said, 'It's not a Hollywood movie.' I had a few notes on the script that I shared with Chris and Aaron. We all understood we were not doing a Hollywood movie – a whodunnit? We realized, as we were getting in, that we were limiting the financial potential of the movie. In saying that, I never expected or dreamt that the movie became what it became.

As Wachsberger calls it, Summit then took Nolan's script 'on the freeway', beginning with European distributors, selecting companies he felt were best suited to releasing *Memento* in their own territory. Only, at this stage, able to read the script, most came on board on faith alone. 'In Europe, people really dug the screenplay. They thought it was interesting enough. They did not know, for the most part, who Christopher Nolan was. Frankly, I don't think any one of them had seen *Following*.' Japan's Amuse Pictures, he notes, was also another distributor that showed interest from the early stages, although most of the deals were not signed until production was under way.

Surprisingly candid for a man who works in Hollywood, Wachs-berger admits – while being satisfied with most of the distributors he signed deals with – not all were the best choices. 'Generally speaking, we hit our target. We went to the right place, but that is not to say we didn't make some mistakes, and misjudgements, with *Memento*, on a pre-sales basis. There were some territories where we could've done better, but very few.'

Italy – the film's rights eventually secured by CDE – proved a par-ticularly tough market to crack. 'It's such a strange market, where specialized movies are concerned. It's a star-driven country, it's a television-driven market, so therefore you feel more secure to go to television with names,' says Wachsberger. Meanwhile, Alexis Lloyd, who was in charge of Pathé in the UK at the time, was one of several to offer advice. 'He really understood the screenplay. He had a tendency to want to be a little too much involved on the creative side! This can happen – you ask someone to read a screenplay to see if they want to buy a movie or not, and they send you back script notes.'

Memento, of course, featured Guy Pearce, more an actor than a star, and here due to be disguised with a crop of blonde hair. What helped the film, internationally, was the inclusion of Carrie-Anne Moss, following her appearance in the Wachowski brothers' *The Matrix*. By the time the cameras rolled in August 1999, over 50 per cent of the ultimate number of distributors who would release the film abroad were signed on. For those that remained, a promo was cut – later to be used as a template for the trailer itself – to show those that had read the script just what the film would look like, visually. 'Chris was very helpful in helping us put together a promo reel, in giving us access to material before he had even done his first cut,' says Wachsberger.

The reel was shown in October 1999 in Milan, just as production on the film came to a close in California, at the MIFED marketplace, partly to reassure those that had already invested in the project that it was looking good. By this point, the pre-sales had already covered the $4.5 million budget. 'We were not spending a lot of money doing this movie,' says Wachsberger, 'so it wasn't that the target number was astronomical or so far-fetched that we needed huge numbers.' The last territory to be sold was Australia (though their April 2001 release date preceded the likes of Thailand and South Korea), and the film – while cut – had not yet even been screened. Other territories already sold to included Austria, Benelux, Bulgaria, Canada, Czech Republic,

Denmark, Germany, Greece, Hong Kong, Hungary, Iceland, Israel, Latin America, the Middle East, New Zealand, the Philippines, Poland, Portugal, Russia, Sweden, Finland, Norway, South Africa, Spain, Singapore, Switzerland, Turkey and Thailand.

Taking *Memento* on the festival circuit, before it ever reached any of these territories, proved vital to the film's ultimate worldwide success. Having taken *Following* through some low-key festivals – San Francisco, Edinburgh, Vienna and Dinard, among others – it was obvious that a similarly difficult film such as *Memento* would have to establish a rapport with festival audiences before standing any chance of making it in the marketplace. That said, everyone also knew that – with a cast that included Guy Pearce and Carrie-Anne Moss – the spotlight was going to shine on the film that much more.

'With *Following*, our first festival was at San Francisco, and there wasn't really as much at stake,' says Emma Thomas:

> Obviously, we wanted the film to do well, but we didn't have financiers that had spent enormous amounts of money on the film, waiting to see how it would do. With *Following*, it was Chris's film. For all of us, it was almost enough to watch the film with an audience. It was so far from what we'd been thinking about when we had been making the film on Tottenham Court Road three years previously. With *Memento*, Newmarket had not only put themselves on the line, creatively, but they had put a lot of money into it.

Set for its European bow at the Venice Film Festival, before engagements in France at the Deauville Festival of American Film and at the Toronto Film Festival in Canada, the momentum for *Memento* truly began. 'The film always felt European to me,' says Todd. 'It reminded me of some of the more interesting films from there. Slow but psychological movies. More intelligent films play better in Europe. The art of cinema is more appreciated there.'

Making its première in the Dreams and Visions sidebar at Venice, the film received a standing ovation after its first screening. Emma Thomas remembers that day as one of the most stressful in her life:

> The ovation was amazing. Because it was an audience reading the subtitles, there was a lot less laughter – so there was much more tension. You're listening to every movement that the audience is making. We got to the end, and I suddenly remembered that

somebody had told me the day before that audiences in Venice can boo films or do that slow-clap thing. The film ends very abruptly anyway, and there was suddenly this moment of shock within the audience, and then a huge roar as they stood up and gave Chris an ovation. But for that one moment . . .

Aaron Ryder, who had been with the project almost as long as Chris and Emma, was jubilant. 'That week in Venice was probably one of the best in my life. You have to remember in March we'd shown it to US distributors, who had passed. So from March to September, we had no idea what we were going to do. When we went to Venice, and had that reaction, it was incredibly vindicating.'

Giddy with excitement, as Jonah Nolan recalls, they had succeeded: subtitles and frequent cell-phone interruptions aside, the film had won over an Italian audience. 'We were all so happy that the film could work and succeed on its own terms, even in a foreign language,' says Jonah. 'So Chris went straight to the press conference and spilled the beans.' In front of a packed press conference, in front of the world's media, Nolan proceeded to reveal to the assembled journalists his opinions on the film.

'I was flabbergasted that he did that,' recalls Jonah:

I thought he was on the same page as I was. I took him aside afterwards and said, 'Well obviously it's your film, but I don't think there's any mileage in telling people what you think.' You can post-script that with: 'Well, that's just my interpretation,' but no one will give a shit. As much as we're familiar with the concept of divorcing the artist from the art, it's still a hierarchical permutation. But it certainly hadn't occurred to me that anyone would be particularly interested in knowing what the film was about. Until then, it had been a personal group effort to make this thing and get it out there. We suddenly realized, walking out into the streaming daylight of the Venice Film Festival, with Italians milling around arguing with each other about what the hell happened, that we held the bag on this one. People would want to know what happened.

Chris concedes that his brother was right when it came to the public being all too willing to 'see the film-maker with the answer', and for his following encounters with the press he set out to dissociate himself from any definitive interpretation of the film. Yet, he views his actions at the Venice press conference in another light, believing he had given different people different honest answers:

> When you're at a press conference, and someone's asking a question, you go ahead and answer it whatever way you feel is appropriate. The answer I gave to somebody who's really paying attention, somebody who's really desperate for an answer to the truth of the film, they can extrapolate from the answer what was true or not for the film if they wanted to. But at the same time, there was nothing to hold me to that answer! The point is the ambiguity, the point is the uncertainty. You can never know anything for sure, and you have to choose what you believe.

Even the film-makers themselves were still in debate over the film's meaning. That night, everyone from the *Memento* posse in Venice – including Guy Pearce, who had flown in from Ireland, where he was filming Kevin Reynold's *The Count of Monte Cristo* – went to dinner. The conversation turned to the ending. 'We had a two-hour argument,' recalls Jennifer. 'I couldn't believe we were still debating it, a year after we'd shot the film.' Chris marvelled at the fact that those who had spent three years making the film still contested the film's outcome. 'That's a rather unusual thing,' he says. 'You know what's interesting about the ending to the film? Some people see it as incredibly tidy and tight and complete. Some see it as amazingly ambiguous and loose-ended.'

Within a day, everyone headed off for the less-than-sunny climes of Normandy, for Deauville's Festival of American Film – the first public screening in France, and it was not at the Cannes Film Festival. Advised by their French distributor UGC to wait for this laid-back cinematic showcase, the decision to do so now seems wise, with the film taking the Critics' Prize and tying with *Boiler Room* (another Team Todd production) for the Jury Special Prize. Rejected by the Cannes committee for both the Director's Fortnight and main competition, Newmarket decided against accepting the offer of a slot in the 'Un Certain Regard' strand. 'The folks at Un Certain Regard did enjoy the film, but we thought it may not suit the film best,' says Aaron Ryder. 'So we decided to wait for Venice and Deauville. We had our hopes set on main competition, and when we didn't get into that, we just wanted to wait.'

When the gang flew back across the Atlantic for the Toronto Film

Festival, Bob Berney was able to orchestrate a full US press junket. Utilizing PR company Rogers and Cowan, he saw it as a tremendous opportunity to kickstart the film's word-of-mouth. 'That's a great place to do it, because everybody's there anyway,' says Berney. 'Particularly for North America. Toronto has all the regional journalists: coverage from Dallas and Milwaukee, San Francisco, wherever. We had an amazing screening, and some of the key exhibitors were there. We knew the critical success was coming from Venice, but Toronto was certainly the groundswell for the film's word-of-mouth.'

Berney was also able to make his first contact with US exhibitors (with others catching the film in Sundance later on). The response was very encouraging. 'I met some of the most important figures right there. Particularly Dan Talbot, from Lincoln Plaza Cinemas, one of the most influential theatre owners in the country. He was actually the first one to call me immediately after the screening.'

The early release in the UK (20 October 2000), France (11 October 2000) and Switzerland (October 2000) meant that, for once, a US-set film, backed by an American company, would open in Europe first. 'We released it in Europe because we'd pre-sold the film,' says Ryder. 'Unlike the US distributors, Pathé and UGC loved the movie. They were truly supportive of it, and they wanted to release it earlier, and I'm glad they did – because it started that word-of-mouth.'

Todd herself would later witness this word-of-mouth in full effect. On holiday in Kenya over Christmas 2000, she encountered a fan of the film. 'I was sitting having dinner one night, and this 15-year-old French girl said, 'Oh, you're in the film business? I saw this great film, Memento!' I thought it was rather ironic that none of my friends [in America] had seen it, but I was sitting in Kenya with a French girl who had.'

With the UK release coinciding with the film opening the Raindance Film Festival (the more independent-minded annual precursor to the London Film Festival), Nolan was paid homage to, in a sense, by the festival organizers. Not only was Memento given a prime slot, but Following – despite it being a year since it had been briefly released in London – was screened too. It was surely recognition for a director whose two films – one shot on weekends, the other self-distributed – truly embodied the spirit of independent cinema.

By January, Memento was on the last leg of its festival tour, arriving at the Sundance Film Festival. Despite the film having been launched in

Europe, the festival was more than happy to invite *Memento* to make its American debut. Bizarrely, as Joe Pantoliano points out, there was some cross-over. 'Some of my friends who came from England to the festival had been watching the movie on the airplane!' Yet more press interviews were held, one Berney called 'a fast-breaking press junket', which would yet again stir up media awareness in North America of the film, prior to the March release. For Nolan, he had come full circle, making the transition from Slamdance rebel to Sundance winner. *Memento* won Nolan the Waldo Salt prize for screenwriting, an award claimed in recent years by the likes of esteemed playwright Kenneth Lonergan, Stanley Tucci and Tom DeCillo. Already voted the British Screenwriter of the Year by the London Film Critics, Nolan says he was delighted at winning the prize, though finds the notion of competing as film-makers absurd. 'We were there competing with [John Cameron Mitchell's drag story] *Hedwig and the Angry Inch*! To me, it's very gratifying for someone to like your work, but at the same time, it's quite a strange concept.'

Since Sundance, *Memento* has gone on to claim several more awards. It tied with David Lynch's *Mulholland Drive* for Best Picture, as voted for by the OFCS (Online Film Critics Society), it was awarded the accolade outright by both the LVFCS (Las Vegas Film Critics Society) and the Toronto Film Critics Association. All three of the aforementioned also gave Nolan Best Screenplay, alongside the more prestigious LAFCA (Los Angeles Film Critics Socity) and the AFI (American Film Institue). While Pearce is the only *Memento* actor to so far receive an award (from the LVFCS), at the time of going to press, Carrie-Anne Moss had been nominated for Best Supporting Actress at the Independent Spirit Awards. With *Memento* competing in four other categories (Best Picture, Best Screenplay, Best Director and Best Cinematography), Nolan also finds himself up for a Golden Globe for Best Screenplay.

Sundance did provide one great surprise for actor Larry Holden, who saw the film for the first time at a packed screening. Having worked out at the gym for three weeks solid prior to the shoot to shed some pounds to play drug dealer Jimmy, he was most perturbed when he saw the Polaroid depicting his dead body. 'There's this close-up of my recently "deceased" body and it looks nothing fucking like me!' The actual Polaroid taken on set of Holden had to be re-shot on a day when the actor wasn't available, meaning a body double – less trim than Jimmy – was used. 'Afterwards, in the lobby, Chris and

Emma were laughing hysterically at the look on my face,' he recalls with a grimace. 'They probably just didn't want to pay me for an extra day, the bastards – and they had some poor sod with this big, bloated, whiter-than-mine gut lay on the fucking floor and act dead.'

www.otnemem.com and the marketing of *Memento*

Who can doubt the power of the Internet as a marketing tool in the wake of *The Blair Witch Project*? The site – which dug into the back-story of the film, inventing the myth of the Blair Witch, and teasing film-goers with notions of truth versus fiction – undoubtedly contributed significantly to the buzz that surrounded Daniel Myrick and Eduardo Sanchez's $30,000 camp-fire spook story. By the time it hit the cinemas, web-users worldwide were titillated enough to come out in their droves. Undoubtedly a watershed moment, it forced Hollywood studios to re-evaluate the way they use the Internet. No longer will a glorified menu with pictures suffice. Already, Warner Brothers have taken up the challenge, producing a massive on-line campaign for Steven Spielberg's *A.I.*, allowing the user to surf through a number of subject-related sites. Stimulating interest in artificial intelligence in a broader context, it's also the perfect way to ensnare the interest of web-users in the run-up to the film's release.

'We always knew we wanted something a little more innovative,' says Jonah Nolan, who was chiefly responsible for the design of *Memento*'s website, www.otnemem.com:

We knew we wanted something that would set us apart from all the other low-budget crime thrillers that the market had been recently flooded with. Despite the fact the film was unique in its own right, we wanted the publicity material to match the film. We didn't want to do the *Blair Witch* thing of trying to convince you it was a real story; at the same time, I didn't want any reference on the site itself – at least in the beginning – showing that it wasn't real. Not saying it's a movie, in other words. So there are no credits on the original version of the website.

Serving as an illuminating book-end – together with Jonah's original short story – for the film itself, the *Memento* site begins with the line: 'Some memories are best forgotten.' From this the word 'Memento' is picked out, and a snatch of Leonard's dialogue – 'The world doesn't just disappear when you close your eyes' – is then heard alongside the

67

sound of Teddy's scream in reverse. We are then taken to the home-page, and confronted with a newspaper article (undated) that has the headline: 'Photograph Sparks Murder Investigation'. The standfirst below adds: 'Motel Customer Disappears; Leaves Suspicious Photograph, Gun, Documents and Questions'. The story itself details Leonard's disappearance from the Discount Inn, after killing Teddy. There is even a quote from Burt, calling him 'polite but weird, forgetful'. Linking back to Jonah's short story, we are told that a man by the same name escaped from a Bay-area psychiatric facility in September 1998. From this article, a number of key words are highlighted. Selecting each one takes you further back into Leonard's story, mixing first-person handwritten notes to himself (as the short story will do) with documents, such as police reports, diagrams and Polaroids.

In no particular order, the sub-sections are as follows:

Questions: We hear Teddy say: 'Maybe you should start investigating yourself,' before seeing a scrap of paper with the words: 'Who did I kill?' on it.

Body: 'I'm going to kill him,' says Leonard, before we see a picture of Teddy, spliced with pictures of Leonard's wife.

Local: A series of clips relating to Natalie, who we hear ask Leonard: 'The next time you see me, will you remember me?' We then cut from a picture of the Polaroid of her to the beer mat, and then the pharmacy bag with the meeting crayoned over it, and finally to the photocopy of Teddy's licence plate.

Suspicious: Leonard's comment after photographing Natalie – 'Something to remember you by' – is heard before we see a picture of him tattooing his own arm. A handwritten note tells him to find 'a more permanent way of writing things down', followed by pictures of broken biros, a note telling him to shave and a copy of the licence-plate number, which he will ultimately record on himself, leading him to kill Teddy.

Leonard: After we hear Leonard tell Burt: 'If we talk for too long, I'll forget how we started,' we cut to a newspaper clipping, detailing the original break-in. Significantly, a number of details are inked out, but we learn that 'Mrs Shelby had been sexually assaulted and received a number of serious injuries to her head, neck and upper body.' No mention of her supposed death is made. After pictures of Mrs Shelby, two handwritten notes follow. The first is provocative: 'She's gone, Leonard. Gone for good. You're the only one left. But there isn't much left of you, is there? He took that too.' The second asks Leonard to remember Sammy Jankis, commenting on the irony of Leonard not believing Sammy's story.

Revenge: Natalie tells Leonard, 'Even if you get revenge, you're not going to remember it. You're not even gonna know it happened.' We cut to a police report, detailing the death of one of the intruders, on 24 February 1997. A handwritten note then urges Leonard to find the other intruder. A second scrap calls him 'a coward'. A third, in a direct repetition of a segment of Jonah's short story, says the only consequence of avenging his wife's death will be imprisonment in a 'little room', adding, 'in case you hadn't noticed, that's exactly where you're already at'. We are then shown a psychiatrist's report (dated 17 September 1998), that states it has been 'a strange and troubling week in Leonard's recovery' as he has learned to distrust his attendants. It also talks of his journal, which contains self-penned notes inciting himself to escape. We then switch to a note listing four facts about John G.

Forgetful: The most extensive segment. We first hear Natalie ask: 'What's the last thing that you do remember?' We cut to a picture of a body, with contusions – like Leonard's – marked on the diagram, and his diagnosis, 'Extreme Head Trauma: Apparent Disorientation, Memory Lapses'. A note tells him, rather ambiguously, that his wife 'has gone for good . . . so you've got to stop looking for her'. A further psychiatric report, dated 16 Jauary 1998, tells us Leonard is an 'allegedly mentally sick person'. Leonard is admitted to the institution as a ward of the state, with a high level of 'memory disruption'. A doctor's report indicates Leonard forgot his examiner's name seven times in an hour and a half before demanding to see his wife. A handwritten note goads him, saying all the medical specialists can hope to do is rehabilitate him. A report, dated 4 April 1998, indicates he has developed a keen interest in crossword puzzles – as also shown in the short story – while his 'cognitive-amnesiac period remains at roughly fifteen minutes, although this greatly shortened by anxiety'. Finally, another self-penned scrap says the doctors would put him in a straitjacket if they knew what would make his pain go away – that is, revenge.

Without ever being explicit, the site sets out to provide background details to Leonard, previous to the events of the film, alongside a hint that Leonard will have moved on to another motel and another revenge-killing. Alongside the short story (see Appendix), the details presented here set out to show how Leonard escaped from the institution, and began this perpetual cycle of revenge. Establishing the film in a broader context, Jonah believes the site echoes a number of the film's themes:

> I don't want to get too postmodern, but it is interesting because you can look at the story and then the film, and in these conflicting narratives, it's two different people trying to tell the same story. Given the subject matter, that's an interesting point: the way that my version of events conflict with my brother's. I ran most of the ideas for the website past him, but he gave me a long leash to play with in terms of manipulating his characters and feeding them back into the story that I'd come up with. There's no reference in the film, other than a cut-away shot that lasts three-tenths of a second, of Leonard actually being in a mental asylum himself. The story and the website are primarily about that.

For Jonah, the site, to some extent, represented the conclusion to what he set out to do with the original short story that inspired the film. As he points out, the website can't be read like a book, but more resembles the way we would read a magazine, skipping back and forth, depending on what we were first drawn to. A better analogy – something he hoped to achieve for the original story – is a deck of cards. Intending to write the short from a number of different perspectives, Jonah hoped 'each reader would shuffle the pages before making their way into a completely fractured, random narrative'. While, much to Chris's annoyance, he never followed through with this idea, the opportunity to similarly piece together Leonard's back-story, via an arbitrarily ordered set of documents, is provided by the website.

'One of the things I tried to do with the website is allow you to assemble these police reports, medical documents, newspaper stories, and see if you have any idea what happened,' says Jonah:

> But you'll have four or five different accounts of where you can look at the material of the website and come up with a number of events. The idea that it's up to the audience to try and put together

a version of events to understand what happened . . . what I find fascinating is the reluctance of some people to do that. There is an obsession with knowing what happened. This is why we're fascinated with the Kennedy assassination. We're never gonna know, never. It was thirty years ago, and there are hundreds of different points of view. Even with it on film, we've no idea what happened.

Jonah volunteered to design the site after it was discovered Internet design companies (still luxuriating in the URL boom, before the dot.com bubble burst) were charging inflated prices for their work. Teaming up with a New York-based friend Marko Andrus, who ran a website company himself, Jonah busied himself learning the various software packages needed to create a home page. 'I had taken a computer science course in college and realized that what most clients of Internet companies don't realize is that this stuff is remarkably easy to put together. It took just a couple of hours to learn the programmes.'

More taxing, it seemed, was the creation of the materials ultimately scanned in for the site. Using just a computer, a Polaroid camera and various dummy forms he had pinched from the props department on set, Jonah set about re-creating documents evidencing Leonard's existence from his time in the asylum. A part-time security guard, during his time studying at Georgetown University in Washington DC, Jonah had spent his nights checking IDs at the front desk, and ferrying drunks home across campus. 'As all rent-a-cops do, you get into the idea that you're out there to keep an eye out for serious crime. You watch all these crime TV shows as a kid, and on the spot you can conjure up the language of the rigmarole of amateur police-work,' he says. 'Every night, I would have to fill out a log report, so I got very interested for a while in the bureaucracy of crime prevention – and how boring it is.'

Printing out forms, and tearing them into scraps, his time spent on-set with Cindy Evans, and her assistant costume designers, helped enormously when it came to ageing the materials. 'The actual work of putting it on the web was peanuts compared to getting it together and making it look dirty, and fucked-up and old and interesting,' he recalls. 'I would ride around the subway, rubbing Polaroids against the roof of the subway car. I would crumple them up, and carry them around in my pocket, trying to get them to age.'

Simultaneously, Jonah also wrote the e-mails that fans could receive

71

as if from Leonard himself. An approach already used for the marketing of Mary Harron's *American Psycho* (Patrick Bateman's despatches were penned by Bret Easton Ellis himself), letters were sent out from Leonard playing on the notions already suggested by story and screenplay. Addressed to John G., they have been written three years on (so we are told) from the initial assault, with Leonard claiming to be on his attacker's trail: 'I'm going to kill you like I killed your friend.' Interestingly, within letter number 3, there is a wry little rebuttal to a question that bothered some fans of the film: how Leonard recalls his own memory loss. 'Try this one: "How does a man with no memory remember his own condition?" But I don't waste my time with philosophical questions any more, John, at least, I don't think so.' In the fourth letter, we get further insight into Leonard's existence – 'For me, every place is new, all the time. This town doesn't look familiar. I don't even know what it's called, don't know how long I've been here, don't know how long I'm going to stay . . . [I'm] like a road show, going from town to town, stuck in the first act.' Leonard's morality is also called into question, as he questions his desire for revenge, 'a tough proposition', as he terms it. 'Part of me worries what I'm doing is wrong. But I can't do anything about it, John, you're talking to the wrong guy.' Curiously, at the end of letter number 5, Leonard says to John G.: 'You want to know why I'm really writing to you? I think I wanted to apologize.' It is as if Leonard is guilt-ridden about his intent.

While responsible for creating much of this extensive back-history, Jonah is happy to downplay the importance of reading his story, and viewing the site, before seeing the film itself. 'I'm not big on the idea of films needing to be set in a context. I think Chris has accomplished this. You can just see the film and be very happy with that. Chris is not a film-maker who is reliant on the merchandise, the T-shirts, the action figures, the dime novels. He has made a world that functions completely independently of my story and the website. But I do think it's interesting to look at all three together.'

Chris, on the other hand, is convinced of the value of establishing a film in a universe that extends beyond the parameters of the film:

What the *Blair Witch* people got absolutely right, which I thought was really cool, was if you really looked at the website before you went to see the film, you actually got a lot more out of the film. It creates a larger experience than film-makers have to do. I recently got to meet the Wachowski brothers, who are working on the sequels to *The Matrix* – of which they would tell me nothing! – but they are very clearly taking into account the bigger multimedia picture, in terms of the offshoots that any big film generates. If you can do it yourself, and not just hand it to a PR department which doesn't add anything creative, you can increase people's understanding of the film, allowing them to re-experience it again.

With Jonah and Chris having created the site off their own backs, the arrival of Bob Berney – when Newmarket decided to distribute the film themselves – galvanized their hard work, as he quickly realized the value of their efforts. 'My contribution was to take advantage of the organic marketing that was already in place,' says Berney:

> This is what the bigger studios sometimes miss; they have to do their own thing no matter what, which has to fit a certain formula. When I met Jonah, and looked at the site he had already made for the film, I thought we had to go with this. I had to make sure it got out there and we marketed that site. *Memento* recognized the power of what's already there. Chris and Jonah already had a really good sense of the audience for the film. Sometimes, it's a simple thing – the key marketing elements are there, and you just to have to take advantage of them. You don't have to re-invent. They felt very strongly about who they made the film for. I said, 'Let's enhance and build on this.'

Passing out postcards at the Toronto festival, which were designed in the shape of a Polaroid with an 'obscure picture of Guy' on the front and just the word 'otnemem' printed on the back, the website began receiving hits straight away, members of the public intrigued by what they saw.

'The website didn't have cast lists,' says Berney. 'It wasn't like you were fooling everybody; people knew what it was. We tried to have a building strategy. The best web stuff is always viral, it spreads. Everyone knows it's a promotion, but if you make it fun and smart, people enjoy being in on it, and telling each other about it. We tried to let it build and not overdo it.'

Meanwhile, with little p&a budget to speak of, other unconventional and innovative methods were dreamed up to promote the film. Newmarket hired New York-based press company Electric Artists to randomly bulk-mail Polaroids to unsuspecting home-owners. Each simply depicted the shot of a topless and blood-smeared Leonard pointing to his chest after reputedly killing John G. 'They'd sent out a boat-load of these things,' says Ryder. 'I got a call one day from a woman who had no idea what this was. All it said on it was "Memento" spelt backwards – otnemem. That was it – and, of course, a picture of a half-naked, bloody man pointing at his chest. She assumed she was being stalked, and she filed a report. The police traced it back, and found out it was a movie. That grass-roots publicity really helped us.'

With no commercial spots lined up for network television in the US, owing to the expense, cheaper cable channels – like Bravo and A&E – were targeted for short 15- and 30-second trailers. With Newmarket now acting as distributor, it meant that Nolan and Team Todd were afforded a rare luxury for film-makers – remaining hands-on during the film's marketing campaign. 'Jonah and I were very instrumental in cutting our first trailer,' recalls Chris. 'We cut a foreign one and a domestic one. For the foreign one, which played in England, Jonah and I went to the edit suite, and talked to the editor.'

Berney found himself heavily involved in shaping the trailer and TV spots, hiring LA-based company Global Dog House to cut them. 'What I do is try to find the right editor for the film. I had a really good feeling that Steve Perani, at Global Dog House, would come up with an unusual trailer that sold the film. It was great. He made a really good go at it. We worked with the Newmarket people, and with Chris Nolan and the Todds. Everybody worked together on it.'

The finished trailer, at the time of writing still available to view on-line, indeed captures the mood of the film very well. Opening with a shot of the Polaroid camera sucking the photo back into the machine, we are immediately introduced to Leonard, as he references his 'condition' to both Teddy and Natalie. Shots of him combating the problem, such as writing on the Polaroids, are cut alongside title-cards detailing the names of the three actors; within seconds, though, two major principals are noted. Teddy tells Leonard: 'You do not know who you are,' blatantly indicating that the protagonist is not to be fully trusted. This is followed by Burt's use of the word 'backwards', warning us of the film's structure, which precedes a shot of Teddy's blood running up the wall. We are then introduced to the idea that Leonard is trying to find his wife's killer – 'You wander round playing detective' – and a number of action sequences are cut together, before Teddy ('Maybe you should start investigating yourself') and Natalie ('You can never know any-thing for sure') remind us that this is a film that cannot be taken at face value. A shot of Mrs Jankis's watch being re-wound reminds us that time, in the film, will be played out backwards, before the pace of the trailer accelerates with a number of speedy shots of Teddy's death. It closes with Leonard in voice-over – 'The world just doesn't disappear when you close your eyes,' fading to the word 'Memento'.

Unlike studios, though, who are able to attach trailers to films of theirs currently playing, Newmarket had no other project to attach *Memento* to. It meant Berney having to go to exhibitors, screen the trailer and negotiate:

> They responded really well to the trailer, and thought it was such a powerful piece, that they put it up early, over the Christmas play-time, which is highly unusual. Usually, you get trailers six weeks in advance. It's tough for an independent distributor to get them up at Christmas for Spring. I think they felt the film was a special film right away. Also, as an independent distributor, the fact that we had the materials ready that early – I don't think they'd seen that. We were really aggressive in trying to get this stuff completed in time to really promote the film. A lot of independents don't have the time or money to do that.

At the same time, the trailer was sent to key websites like Yahoo and MSN, sites inundated with requests by film companies to showcase their films. Response was so strong that Berney was swamped with demands for exclusivity on the trailer. 'They were all putting it right at the front of their home pages.' With the domestic trailer running to around 2 mins 10 secs, the variety of TV spots created utilized the same graphics, with the 'letters evolving' as Berney puts it, but focused on different parts of the main trailer, each spot using a separate strand. Review spots, once the critics had seen the film, were also created, with quotes woven through the thirty seconds.

By this point, though, Nolan himself was tired. 'At the time, I was very weary of the film. I'd been working on it for a very long time, thinking, "Oh, Gosh, now we're gonna have to carry on pushing it." But I have to say I've found that is the case through my whole career. Increasingly, with every film I've made, I've had more people helping me out, bringing things to the table. But at the end of the day, nobody cares about or understands the film as much as I do. I have to push it.'

Basic newspaper ads on the week of the US release were run in the *LA* and *New York Times*, though even this was limited, given the lack of publicity funds. 'I remember we were debating do we run a full page, or a quarter page on the day the film was released,' says Todd. 'For this we were all very involved. Chris, Emma, Bob Berney and Suzanne and I would all get in a room together. We would talk about the poster, the print ads, the quotes. We all conceptually had the idea that the Polaroids should be used. There's one foreign poster where you see him with the tattoos, with Carrie-Anne behind him. But here we didn't want to show the tattoos; we wanted to keep it as a surprise.'

Nolan was given final say in how he wanted the US poster, designed by a company called Crew, to appear:

They showed me an enormous raft of ideas, which were all beautifully produced, but all along the lines of what you would expect: looking like *Se7en*, with lots of layered imagery, and text and ripped-up pictures. Within that, they had a couple of interesting ideas, one of which was recursion – the picture within the picture – that they'd crafted after they'd seen the film. All the other stuff was just from seeing the trailer. I thought it was very apt. Originally it was just Guy within Guy within Guy; I think it was me who came up with the idea of putting Carrie-Anne inside, so that it was a double loop, which I thought was very interesting.

One of the more innovative advertising campaigns came from Pathé distribution in the UK. Targeting film-savvy publications like *Time Out*, they found an unusual way to highlight critics' quotes. A Polaroid snapshot was taken of each journalist, and printed along the border of the poster itself, with their quotes inscribed on the base of the photo. This was not something repeated in America. 'The US critics were a little bit more shy!' remarks Ryder. 'I think it's all the bad reviews they give people – they wanted to hide behind their anonymity. But we studied everything Pathé were doing; they released the film before we did, and everything that worked for them, we stole!'

Meanwhile, following the junkets already held in Venice, Deauville, Toronto and Sundance, press days were held in New York and Los Angeles just a week prior to the release, handled by experienced PR company MPRN. 'I brought on aggressive teams, and tried to put them all together with a strategy to make it cohesive and build on what Chris and Jonah had discovered,' says Berney. 'Our initial approach was to get the long-lead film publications, and film-writers, by interesting them in the director and the story. Then we targeted *People* magazine, and talk shows like *The Today Show*, with the star-sell.' All the key cast members were available, in LA, and willing to help promote the movie: Guy Pearce was shooting *The Time Machine*, Carrie-Anne Moss training for *The Matrix* sequels and Joe Pantoliano in pre-production on his aborted directorial debut *Just Like Mona*. 'Guy and Carrie-Anne, after the junket, had to go off to other films, but Joey continued to do stuff for months,' recalls Berney. 'He's the hardest-working man in show business. He helped us endlessly publicity-wise. He was on radio talk shows, TV shows, on and on. Even a few weeks ago, he went on the Howard Stern show talking about it.'

As far as Pantoliano was concerned, with his contract offering a share of the back-end profits, he was just protecting his investment. As far back as the first screening of the movie – with Nolan, Carrie-Anne Moss, Guy Pearce, and sundry friends – Pantoliano had campaigned to have the movie released in Europe first, believing the European critics would understand the film – a reasoning that proved instinctual. 'I remember being concerned by the genre of the film, and thinking, "What American audience is going to have the patience to sit through this?"' he says. During the LA press junket, he suddenly realized: college kids.

> I said to Aaron: 'Y'know, I think we're ignoring a whole market, with college kids. I think college kids would really enjoy dissecting a movie like this.' At that point they had no money to release the movie. Three days later he called me up and said, 'The good news is, we're taking your advice. The bad news is, you leave Thursday.' They sent me everywhere: Detroit, Boston, Chicago, St. Louis . . . I was going to radio stations, television stations, getting on a plane. Carrie-Anne was working, Guy was working . . . and I had a window in my schedule for *The Sopranos*. I think it was the success of that that helped. Everything lucked out; all the stars aligned.

Chapter 3

'Now . . . where was I?'
Assembling *Memento*

The edit

Dody Dorn first encountered Chris Nolan in an elevator, on the way up to her meeting with him. She had met *Memento*'s newly appointed production designer Patti Podesta before, though never worked with her, and when the position of editor was under discussion, Podesta pointed out her name to Nolan on the shortlist.

'Our first meeting was very odd,' Dorn recalls:

> I got into this elevator, and this guy got in. We rode up in silence, and you know how it is in elevators, right? At the top, just as the doors are opening, this other person says, 'You wouldn't happen to be Dody Dorn, would you?' I said, 'Well, at least we've had a silent moment together.' From there, it was a very pleasant meeting. And that's important. When you get into an editing room with a director, you're there for a long time, hours, days, weeks and even months. So you have to get along. It's really important.

She had already taken the time to watch *Following*, to get a sense of where Nolan was coming from. 'I was very impressed [by the editing]. It was conceptualized very neatly,' she says. A fan of the film's use of visual clues to aid the viewer in re-ordering the story chronology, it was something Dorn saw as 'very bold'. It would also be something Nolan would return to in *Memento*, using the scratches on Leonard's face as a marker-point for the time-line, rather than indicating the passing of day or night. 'He's very attached to that idea, and I think he uses it really well. Sometimes, it works on a subtle level. There are probably people who watch his films and do not necessarily know, but will still get it on a subconscious level.'

Dorn remembers also being impressed by the length of their first discussion; Nolan took the time to get to know her. He also saw her jacked up on coffee, a beverage she had been advised against drinking during business meetings. 'I get really intense when I drink it,' she laughs. 'But we were both offered it, and we both said "Yes". Over the course of the meeting, he saw my personality change. So I figured, if he's seen that, we should get along.' She told him the script was a good read, though added, 'but everybody must tell you that'. He replied, simply: 'Actually, no. Some people don't get it.' After reading the script for the first time, Dorn herself was confused. 'I felt like I better read it again!' she says. She did, another three times. 'I had a lot of questions, but I knew by virtue of the fact that it was daring, that no matter what happened, it was going to be an interesting job. For an editor, it was a dream come true: up front, to be told that you're part of the narrative.'

Dorn was fascinated by *Memento*'s bold structure, and the way in which it firmly placed you in Leonard's helpless position. 'It wasn't just a gimmick,' she says. 'Tarantino is the most well known for re-ordering, but I don't always know why he does it; here I really know why. It totally informs the narrative. Every time I watch the film, I experience it differently. That's the beauty of it, that even I can have a different experience. I also really get a lot out of watching an audience react to it. Every time I see the film, the audience is dead silent, sitting up in their seats. You can't afford to miss a second.'

Discussion, at their first meeting, briefly touched on that most infamous of reverse-structured works, Harold Pinter's *Betrayal*. Dorn also drew Chris's attention to an Italo Calvino work, *If on a Winter's Night a Traveller*, which she had read, that reminded her of the script for *Memento*. 'It was a book I never completed because it irritated me! I was so pissed off by being jerked around by this book. I felt frustrated. And it was frustrating to read the script, but I appreciated it. I think that it is [a frustrating film], and I think that is part of its appeal. People have been fed so many stories, which take them by the hand. It's emotional gridlock, in a lot of ways, and I think people appreciate that. You never get that on a film.'

Nolan had already interviewed a number of editors for the job – all of whom he felt would've edited the film just as was envisioned in his script. 'Chris felt that I might help bring another layer,' says Dorn. 'I think he felt that what I would bring would be something different than what he would necessarily have thought. In other words, getting an editor who would add a layer that was not necessarily encompassed in your vision. Even if you don't choose to take that layer on, at least you're being presented with those options.'

Nolan concurs, stating that shot-for-shot he could have edited the picture himself, having put *Following* together. 'That's how I shoot when I'm on set; I'm editing in my mind. I wasn't looking for somebody to enhance that. I was looking for someone who could bring something different; an emotional element.' The film that actually convinced him she was the right editor for the job was Kirby Dick's 1997 documentary, *Sick: The Life and Death of Bob Flanagan, Supermasochist*. A disturbing, yet moving, account of the eponymous – and notorious – performance artist, it depicted in uncensored detail a man who was, until his death in 1996, an 'artist, masochist, and one of the longest living survivors of Cystic Fibrosis'.

'There's a point in which the guy hammers this nail through his penis and blood drips on to the camera,' says Nolan:

> I found myself not being repulsed by that, which, to me, was an incredible thing, and spoke very highly of the editing that had gone into the film. With the director, she had managed to build this portrait of a person in such a beautiful way that you understood him to the degree where you could watch it and not be disgusted. A lot of editors would've opened with that shot and used it for shock value. Somehow, she managed to contextualize it. That seemed to me to be the type of editor I was after: somebody who could understand the audience's emotional response to the character, who was doing sometimes unpalatable things, in the case of Leonard.

A native of LA, Dorn began her career in other areas of film production. A production assistant on a movie-of-the-week about Elvis Presley, she was asked to be the assistant editor on the foreign version. She kept that job title for another four years, though disliked the fact that she learnt nothing creative about the job. She left to work in sound, moving from sound assistant to editor to supervisor, ultimately to work seven days a week for seven months on James Cameron's complex underwater saga *The Abyss*. 'After that, nothing was ever as exciting again,' she says. 'So I went back to picture editing.'

The first project that marked Dorn's return to the picture-edit suite was one that would prepare her mentally for the task of editing *Memento*. Made in Germany, though shot in English, Oliver Hirschbiegel's *Murderous Decisions* was in fact two films telling the same story from two different characters' points of view. Broadcast simultaneously on two different channels, the viewer could switch back and forth between each story. Featuring *Memento*'s Burt himself, Mark Boone, Jr, who by coincidence was lodging with Dorn at the time, the idea – rather than the result – was what counted. 'It was like two different movies,' he says. 'It's the weirdest thing, and it didn't really work.'

Dorn saw it more like an interactive game. 'It was very fun for me to edit. It was pretty complicated. I had to keep two tracks and two pictures in synch. At any point the viewer switched channel, they had to be at the same point in the story. I think I have sort of a precise, almost mathematical mind for this kind of thing; for me, it's just more fuel on the fire for wanting to stay in the room and figure things out.'

One of the first decisions she and Nolan had to make was whether the repeat sequences shown in the film would be additional takes of the same scene. 'We decided very quickly that that was not a wise thing to do,' she says. 'The subtleties of the differences in takes would've been very apparent; the re-interpretation of scenes, via different takes or angles, would've confused the issue. Re-interpretation comes from the knowledge, not the performance. If you take the scene, for example, where Carrie-Anne comes back in the house, if you'd used a different take, her performance might've betrayed more or less of her conniving.'

As it turns out, though, Nolan was interested in mixing exact footage with alternative takes. For example, the scene in the restaurant bathroom, where he tries to wash off the 'Remember Sammy Jankis' tattoo on his hand, is – on its repeat – dupe footage for all shots except the close-up of Pearce's hand. 'It's a very complex mixture, done for all kinds of different reasons – some of which are narrative, some of which are more practical.' He cites also the skid to a halt outside Emma's Tattoos, which is not only two different takes, but two different set-ups. 'On one, you're up a building and the car skids into frame; on the other, you're on the car, and the building skids into frame – that's the most extreme example of the way in which things are different. In the one, it's the beginning of the scene, and your awareness of the scene begins with the fact that you've stopped outside a tattoo parlour. The next time you see it, it's the end of the scene, and your awareness is that you're skidding to a halt, but you don't quite know why and it ends with the fact that you're skidding to a halt – that's a very different function in a way. It has a different feel at the end of the scene as it does at the beginning, by using different takes.'

As Nolan points out, though, his intention was not to disorientate the audience, by using different takes or set-ups. 'We never did it to that extent. There's so much disorientation anyway – more, if anything, for reasons of being true to the idea of memory shifting the perspective slightly, on an event or an image. Presenting it in slightly different ways sometimes seems very true to that idea.'

Dorn began editing the second day after shooting began. She would watch the dailies with the lab rep every morning before watching them again with Chris in the evening. He wanted to see them projected because he had shot in anamorphic, but both had to watch them in silence, as sound is not normally printed at this stage on low-budget features. 'Chris spent most of his time in those dailies, with the DP [Director of Photography], which is as it should be, because they're talking about the next day. But I still had the pleasure of seeing it on a large screen, on film, and knowing whether or not it was in focus.' At lunch, she would visit Chris in his trailer to talk about the material watched from the night before. 'I was visualizing information from him throughout the shooting period,' she says. 'Editing it, for me, was like reading the script for the fifth time. So many things that I had read came to life, and expanded, visually and emotionally. I could understand what was happening in the script; the physical manifestation I read and got, but the emotional quality I only understood when I edited it.'

Dorn's gender, and understanding of the film's emotional core, led her to aid the edit greatly during the sequence where Natalie asks Leonard to truly remember his wife. 'The flashbacks, and the emotion that it creates – I said that I felt that that scene would create a very strong response in female viewers, because every woman wants to have a man feel that way about them. And by the nature of the intensity of it, and the quietness of it, and the choices and images, it helped the level of emotionality.'

While Nolan is reluctant to reduce Dorn's contribution simply to enhancing the characters of Natalie and the wife, he does admit it was useful to have a female perspective on board. '[Dody's work] was also a question of the perspective on Leonard himself, and how we want to view him, relative to the other characters,' he adds. As actor Mark Boone, Jr confirms, it was difficult for Dorn to shake Nolan away from intensifying the spotlight on Leonard. 'She said to me, "I really wanted to be on you more, but Chris kept saying I had to be on Guy!" That was the director's choice, I guess,' he says.

Working first in Glendale, near the soundstage where much of the film was shot, for the four weeks of the shoot, Dorn moved her work to an editing suite at the Universal Studios lot after the film wrapped. Chris joined her a few days after the shoot, and the pair would spend another six weeks before the first working cut was fully assembled. With around 150,000 feet of film shot, Dorn found herself using 135,000 feet – indicating what little waste there had been on the shoot. Using an Avid machine, she was granted more freedom than if starting with a work print – which requires careful consideration before making the first splice. With the Avid, changes are easy to make. 'I'll often try something, and then just insert a line from another take, and watch it through – which I can do very quickly.' While this made things easier, for Dorn the process of editing is all about perspiration.

'You just have to dive in, and keep working, working, until it's right,' she says. 'Sometimes the very first cut is the best one, but not always. You just keep refining.' Certain scenes were close to her first assembly, such as when Sammy kills his wife. Others, ultimately, became radically different from how she first visualized them. Take the scene where Sammy is examined by the doctors. 'I had seen it sort of as a sound gag, and Chris saw it more visually. I included both elements, but it was very different to how it first was. On the page, it's just Sammy gets tested, so what do you do but look at the images and decide what you think will be interesting? Just sitting and staring at the screen will never edit a film!'

Just as Nolan had written the script in the order it appears, so he wanted the editing process to mirror this. 'I just used to always write that way when I was in college,' he says. 'I would never do much of an essay plan, but when I wrote I would basically progress in a very linear fashion. That's the way I've always worked. For me that's the best way to establish the narrative flow, regardless of what the chronology is.'

Editing in the order that the scenes appear on screen was crucial for maintaining a forward-moving sense of rhythm – even though the narrative is heading backwards.

'I wanted to keep the rhythm and logical connection between narrative elements,' says Nolan. 'To achieve the correct flow, you must view things as they come on screen. If you think of an incoming image you're seeing for the first time, that cut-in has a very different effect than the cut-out. On the cut out, your brain is able to extrapolate, so if you see a motion across screen and cut out of it, your brain is able to have an echo of it. It can't do that on the front end; if you take a cut sequence and you just flip it round, the cuts generally won't work.'

Aside from keeping the script in her lap at all times, Dorn used an 'arcane' system to help order the film in her mind. Her assistants Cybele O'Brien and Mike Grant, wrote out three-by-five cards, putting them on the wall, not unlike Leonard's own wall-chart that he uses to map out his investigation. With titles like 'Leonard heats the needle' and 'Sammy accidentally kills his wife', Dorn admits the cards were a source of amusement for her, though she found herself staring at them all day long. 'The three-by-five cards are pretty standard Hollywood vernacular, because lots of editors use them,' she says. 'We also used a colour-coding system, so that we could see on the card whether it [the sequence] was a repeat or not. We also had colour-code for the black-and-white sequences, and the flashbacks. I made a book out of them, sort of like a scrap book, just for fun.'

Dorn also made title banners for each scene, with a scene number, because with the excess of repetitive material, it helped keep her aware of exactly where she was in the film. Like a title above the frame for every inch of the film, it became indispensable. 'The banners were different to the cards,' she says. 'It was something I needed to have for a lot of different reasons.' It confirmed if the material being edited was for the first or second time the viewer would watch the scene, something even Nolan himself needed to know. 'Even Chris says if he were to walk into the film today after it had already started, he wouldn't know where he was in the structure of the film.'

The banners also helped the sound editors – led by Gary Gerlich – who would only ever receive the film broken down in 20-minute increments – which, again, would disorient them as to exactly where they were in the film's time-line. In addition, a chart detailing which parts of the film were being repeated was made for the sound department. Sound effects, such as a dog bark, would also have to be repeated exactly as the footage itself was. 'It never became a headache,' says Dorn. 'The only headache we had was that we had a very short schedule. We had to find a way to get everything the way that it was meant to be in a short amount of time.'

Aiming for a two-hour running time, she and Nolan initially found their first cut ran to around 130 minutes, or at least that's what they shrewdly told Newmarket and the Todds. 'I told them the film was longer than it was, when I showed it to them, so I could then turn round and say I'd cut ten or fifteen minutes. It works quite well! It's not lying. It's the length that everyone wants it to be at the end of the day.' Actually trimming back between eight and ten minutes – it's a move that demonstrates, despite his inexperience at this level, just how well Nolan understands the minds of producers. During the trim, owing to the precise structure of the piece, no actual scenes were lost. 'No narrative material was dropped,' remarks Dorn. 'I'd never worked on a film that had ever done that. All we lost were some tit-bits in the motel room, all around the time he is tattooing himself and breaking the pen. They were not real scenes; they're more like markers. We combined some of those images, so that they became one instead of two. That meant that because all of these repeats were bracketed by black-and-white scenes, we had to lose some of these beats.' Nolan, who says cutting a film where no scenes can be removed is like 'editing with one arm tied behind your back', refers to this process as simply 'tightening up', reducing *Memento* to the bare essentials. 'It was what I did with [editor] Gareth Heal in *Following*, as we were able, because of the structure, to strip things down to the absolute essentials and remove all the padding.'

A certain amount of scene-juggling was also achieved, though due to the precise structure of the script, it was limited. Nolan had already experienced this during the editing stage of *Following*, which used an equally radical form to tell its story:

> When I had written the script, which seemed to work on the page, the feeling was if you're going to use this unconventional structure (such as the three time-lines in *Following*), my impulse at script stage was to teach the reader the structure, to do it very quickly with small scenes, so that in the first ten pages you have an idea of the structure throughout. What I found with *Following* and *Memento*, when you come to watch the film, was that's counter-productive. It becomes too baffling for the audience. The audience has to have a period in which to just connect with characters. With both films, I took a couple of the initial blocks, and combining them, so they run conventionally over two blocks. With *Memento*, there were cut points at the arriving at the derelict building, and I ran that together. It's a longer block of time.

As far as the flashbacks of Leonard's were concerned, Nolan was looking for a method to cut them in, without making them seem obtrusive. Strangely, given that Nolan is often compared to Nicolas Roeg in terms of editing style, it was an altogether more conservative director that influenced him: Alan Parker. Already taken with Parker's use of props as a device to link time-lines in *The Wall* (as seen in *Following*),

Nolan remained impressed with his edit technique on *Angel Heart*. Parker's 1987 *noir*-inflected New Orleans-set story about a private eye on the hunt for a crooner gone AWOL already played a similar game to *Memento*, dealing with issues of identity, but it was the director's rapid-cuts of a character's thoughts that captivated Nolan.

> I was very struck by that at the time, because it's rather daring, yet seamless and easy, in a way. Nicolas Roeg and Sidney Lumet were also doing this, but I wasn't familiar with them at the time, so it would be dishonest of me to say I started from looking at Nic Roeg films, when actually I was sitting there watching *Angel Heart*! That's a very mainstream film, so the grammar of editing has taken on those interesting devices from those older films, so you can do that without completely baffling an audience.

Just as at script stage, and even late on during pre-production, the ending to the film was to prove the most difficult to tackle, starting, as Dorn points out, from the moment Leonard kills Jimmy. 'It was always decided that we would end the film with Guy saying "Now . . . where was I?" But the whole thing with Teddy explaining what was going on; and then Leonard setting himself up to kill Teddy . . . that was really important that everyone understood it. We knew there were multiple interpretations available, but we wanted to make sure that there was one interpretation that followed that.'

Spending another three months in the edit suite refining their initial cut, Dorn insists that healthy debate was a vital part of her relationship with Nolan. 'You have to have a few disagreements; if you don't, it's not right,' she notes:

> It's a constant dialogue. I'm the objective viewpoint. I didn't write the script; I'm only looking at the film itself. It's a mosaic, or a puzzle. The editor is a sponge for the director's ideas. I don't want to say we never argued, but Chris's vision was so clean that I can't come up with any horror stories. Chris was very open; I never felt any kind of an ego thing. There was never any stand-off. Everyone knows that the director will get what he finally wants; but he didn't want someone who said 'Yes' all the time.

Ultimately, through the edit, Nolan achieved the creation of a narrative so complex that even he gets lost in it when re-watching *Memento*. 'It's one of the things I'm proudest of with the film. Even though I have a very good memory for films – I have to, to do my job – and I've seen the film thousands of times, I still get completely lost. If I come into a screening halfway through, I don't know what scene I'm in. That's one of the biggest achievements of the film, from my point of view. The film manages to enter the mind in a way I really hoped it would. The fact you can get so lost in it, is very much a by-product of that.'

The grading and the transfer

One of the problems with shooting on black-and-white film stock is, if it is to be mixed with colour sequences, it has, ultimately, to be printed on colour film stock. Early on, Nolan and his director of photography, Wally Pfister, saw the black-and-white dailies (printed to black-and-white stock), and marvelled at the sharp contrast. 'I had the deep blacks, so I felt I was right on course,' says Pfister. When they were printed to colour, contrast and sharpness was lost, and an unwelcome colour tint was gained. 'It was really a downer,' he adds:

> Chris really accepted it. For me it was such a disappointment. In the end, when we had to print to colour, the lab really were never able to nail the look. You inherently get a colour tinting on it, so we had to choose between a reddish tint or a blueish tint. In the end, we aimed towards the blue, but there are prints out there that erred towards the magenta/red side. That part I accepted; what really hurt me was the loss of contrast. I wasn't able to get those really dark, rich blacks that I was able to get in colour footage.

Paying tribute to his colour timer, Mato Der Avanessian, and dailies timer, Don Capoferri, who worked for company Fotokem, Pfister says they did 'a wonderful job in trying to . . . bring back the rich tones'. Brought back into the production, after his work during the actual shoot, to colour-grade the picture, Pfister admits the time he spent in post-production was sizeable.

'It was a lot on this picture, because of the black-and-white. It's hard to be specific on the amount of time I put into it. We would look at a b/w test on Tuesday, then they would re-print it and we would examine it again on Friday . . . that sort of thing. That took place over a couple of months. Then we put all the black-and-white material together, and timed it all, and then we graded the whole picture.'

The process undertaken once the picture is locked, the colour timing is performed to 'try and match the colours up' across the picture, and iron out any colour defects. Pfister calls the grading 'standard' except for the corrections on the Polaroids. 'You couldn't colour-correct for any imperfections in the Polaroids themselves, because you had other elements within the frame, such as a hand holding the photo. So if you tried to take the magenta out of the Polaroid, the hand would turn green.'

The sound

Sound design is always one of the most fascinating, yet undervalued, contributions to a film. An air of mystery hangs over the process. If Martin Scorsese is to be believed, Frank Warner guarded the work he did on *Raging Bull* to an obsessive degree, hiding from the director the sources of many of the distinctive bone-crunching sounds, even burning the tapes so no one else could use them. There is something to be said, though, for this. Ensuring the sounds remain unique to the film goes some way to ensuring the film's longevity. One of *Memento*'s supervising sound editors is Gary Gerlich, a former pupil of Warner's, who worked with him on *Raging Bull*, as well as *Close Encounters of the Third Kind*. Other credits in his illustrious 25-year career include Hal Ashby's *Being There*, Scorsese's *King of Comedy*, Jan De Bont's *Speed*, and, more recently, both *American Pie* films. Fortunately Gerlich is more revealing than his mentor when it comes to discussing the art of sound design. Based at the Universal lot, working alongside *Memento*'s other Supervising Sound Editor Richard LeGrand, Jr, he was brought onto the project by Dody Dorn, when the *Memento* edit relocated itself to the lot. Both Dorn and Gerlich had worked for Twentieth Century Fox in the past, and – while never on the same film – Dorn was aware of his work. Chris Nolan was happy to listen to her suggestion of Gerlich for the job. 'She has a long history in sound,' he says. 'So she knows far more about it than I do, so I trusted her judgement.'

Gerlich was impressed on their first meeting at the clarity of Nolan's vision. 'As far as explaining what he wants, or conveying to a sound designer what he had in mind, Chris was very specific, but very open. He would want to experience different sounds. I could show them to him, and then talk about it. I loved to work that way. He didn't walk me into going for one specific sound for one specific scene. He gave me an idea of what he wanted for the scene, but then he let me go the next step further, and bring a selection to the sound stage.'

Nolan, as he did with Wally Pfister, used the word 'tactile' to explain to Gerlich the feeling he wanted the sounds to evoke. 'I talked about wanting to feel that we know what everything is made of. You do that both with texture, in a visual sense, but also the sound, really getting the feel of Leonard's words – which is so important to him. It's important in terms of putting the audience in his head, making them experience this world in almost excruciating detail. Every time he would write on a Polaroid you would hear it from that perspective.'

For Nolan, the use of tactile sounds was also the chance to aurally alert the audience to the feel of Leonard's world. As if to emphasize this, Leonard verbalizes it to Natalie: 'I know the feel of the world . . . I know how this wood will sound when I knock . . . I know how this glass will feel when I pick it up . . . Certainties. You think it's knowledge, but it's a kind of memory, the kind you take for granted. I can remember so much. I know the feel of the world.` A celebration of sorts, this is Leonard's demonstration to himself that his 'sense memory', as Nolan terms it, is still working. Another mirror to confirm, in a film full of them.

'That came in quite late to the script and it arose from my discussions with people I was trying to interest in the film,' says Nolan:

> I would sit there and explain how I was going to shoot it; I would say all he can remember is what a ceramic mug feels like, for example. Those memories are very precious, and it's one of the processes of memory that still works for him. It's so instinctive for us, but once you become aware of it in the present, it seems to me that Leonard clings to that as proof of the fact that an enormous amount of his memory is still working. If you remove your short-term memory, you live entirely in this ten-foot-square space, and you live in the room you're in right now. You don't know how you got there, or what's outside.

Given a distinct take on what mood was required, as well as what direction the sounds should head, Gary Gerlich set about devising a series of noises that would resonate with Leonard's own experience. 'We were trying to avoid doing something that would take the audience away from the movie,' he says. 'Sometimes, you get a movie and you might add too many things to it. We were very careful about staying within the mood of the movie, to keep it more intimate and in tune with what the scene was trying to say.'

It was decided that certain elements of the story – characters or locations – would be allotted their own sound. The motel room, during the black-and-white sequences, had a sound unique to that apartment: distant traffic noise, but slowed down, suggesting, if nothing else, the timeless nature of Leonard's existence. 'We called it "empty apartment" – it was ominous-sounding,' says Gerlich. 'We tried to not make it too accurate in terms of what you might expect from outside noise. Chris likes to not try and do too much. The sounds were very precise; not a lot of extra stuff was going on, so it really centres on that character.' Likewise, the noise that surrounds Teddy is a street sound, but more natural, and not too busy. Natalie, at her house, has, according to Gerlich, a less ominous and more realistic note. As for the derelict building, Chris requested a 'desolate, in-the-middle-of-nowhere sound' that was also ominous. Gerlich initially considered using a simple array of sounds, a light wind, the occasional bird and a little traffic – until, that is, he came to work on the piece, where he favoured slowed-down winds, tones and drones. The bathroom-rape scene, however, Chris wanted to be 'jarring, like cutting with a knife', as Gerlich puts it. He used a roar, a train and dry ice to achieve this very grating tone.

While much of the film's intricate sound design is almost subliminal in its usage, it provides a worthy complement to the unsettling mood stirred up by David Julyan's evocative score. At points, it even echoes it, as with the scenes in the derelict building, or in the trailer park chase between Dodd and Leonard. There, Julyan's wailing music, which resembles a siren, is matched by Gerlich's *mélange* of street sounds, led by a car alarm, which escalates in density as the scene gets more frantic.

For the flashback in the restaurant to Leonard's wife, Gerlich showed considerable restraint, drawing as he was from his experience working with Warner on *Raging Bull*. 'We took that sequence, and my idea was to take the sound away from that. When he starts thinking about her, everything goes away to silence. All the background – the café, the street – disappears. We had done it before, on *Raging Bull*, on the fight sequences, when everything just goes away, all you hear are the footsteps. It's a draining of sound, so when you come back to reality it makes it so much more dramatic.'

His innovations didn't stop there. Again for the derelict building, he set out to provide Chris with some of the texture he'd requested. 'I was very careful to look at the condition of the building. I brought it up with Chris. I said: 'Going into a building that has been abandoned for years. Looking at the floors, they're all broken up. I want to do some interesting things.' So I took some broken tiles to the Foley stage, and taped them to the floor, and crunched over them. Chris was very pleased how that turned out.'

Working with a five-man crew below him (Sound Effects Editors William Hooper and Patrick O'Sullivan; Assistant Sound Editor Samuel Webb; Dialogue Editors Walter Spencer and Norval Crutcher III), Gerlich was brought on to the project during the edit, spending six weeks working on the film. Initially shown segments of the film, what is remarkable is that Gerlich did not hear Julyan's score, though he had some idea of the direction it would take, until the final sound mix. Armed with a mini-server and a ProTool editing system, Gerlich was able to bring his selection of sounds to Chris on the sound stage, present him with various options and tweak those chosen. He also had to face the inherent sound problems a film with *Memento*'s repetitious structure presented.

'It was important to keep each sound intact as it replayed again,' he says. 'To make sure that each exact background, each exact footstep, each exact phone ring or whatever, was the way it was before. You build each scene pretty much the same way. It doesn't sound hard, but doing it, everything has to be really precise. Continuity was very important, obviously.'

Gerlich was also responsible for ADR (Additional Dialogue Replacement, where lines unclear from the initial recording are cleaned up). This mainly involved Guy Pearce, who by this point was back in Australia working on Michael Petroni's *Til Human Voices Wake Us*. Achieved using an ISDN line, which delivers the sound perfectly, Pearce was able to take direction from Nolan from the other side of the world. The bulk of the changes were new ideas Nolan wanted to try out for the voice-over that accompanies the black-and-white scenes, with Pearce having to improvise these riffs from Oz.

After the final sound mix, Gerlich estimates there was still one-fifth of his task left to do. 'You always add or tune things up,' he says. 'Once that all gets together, you can really see how things are playing. You may say this sound is too much, so let's take it down and feature the dialogue or the music.' Let's do that then.

The music
A one-bedroom flat in London's Blackheath area is an unlikely place to find the studio facilities where the original music to *Memento* was recorded. But here, in this quiet suburb south-east of the city, is where

composer David Julyan set out to lay down his unsettling score. Set back from the main road, his flat looks out onto a sun-lit grassy enclosure; a poster of *Following* and a postcard for *Memento* adorn his walls, and a copy of the script for *Insomnia* sits at the foot of his bed – visual reminders that Julyan, aside from Emma Thomas, is the only surviving link across Nolan's three films. In one corner is the studio: an Apple Mac, two Roland keyboards, a Soundcraft Mixing Desk and a Roland sampler. Julyan points to a third analogue keyboard, the Ensoniq, and says with pride, 'A lot of the weird atmospheric sounds came out of that.'

Well, that's one way of describing the soundtrack. Comprising sixty-one different musical cues, Julyan's score is entirely synthesized. A self-confessed Vangelis admirer, particularly of his music for Ridley Scott's *Blade Runner*, Julyan's appraisal of the man's work rings equally true of his own. 'Often, there is a criticism that electronic music is a bit cold. I think he [Vangelis] achieved – which a lot of people haven't – electronic music with an emotional feel to it.' Set at the opposite end of the musical scale, so to speak, Julyan's low-key score has none of the near-operatic quality that Vangelis invested into the soundtrack for *Blade Runner*. Yet his work, particularly on *Memento*, has this emotive sound he speaks of. Music to infect you, to slip under your skin, it mixes haunting string sequences with flashes of distorted sound that resemble the beating of a pulse. The result is a soundtrack that embodies Leonard's own tragedy.

'One theme I've always been into is the sense of loss,' says Julyan. 'Often directors will use words to me like "loss" and "yearning", and I think it's a really interesting feeling and emotion; that sense of having lost something, but not knowing what you've lost. Which, bizarrely, is, of course, what *Memento* is about. There came a point after I finished *Memento* that I took a step back and realized that the film was about this theme that I'd always been interested in.'

Julyan, who met Nolan at University College, London in 1993, is not musically trained. A student of astronomy and physics, he spent his weekends dabbling on his parents' keyboard at home, and creating pieces of music on friends' home-based set-ups. 'I then started to think more seriously about it, after some encouragement from friends in bands,' he says. 'Was it actually possible to turn this into a day-job?' Claiming he had no master-plan, or long-held desire to be the next Kurt Cobain, Julyan became interested in 'electronic ambient music', as he calls it. 'I was writing atmospheric stuff anyway at the time, and with the whole chill-out club scene happening, that kind of music was getting more acceptable, or sellable, shall we say. I was sending demo tracks out to record companies, which was probably not the way to get famous. I got a lot of response of "We really like it, but where's the hit single?" No one was prepared to say "We'll give you a deal to make atmospheric ambient music!"'

Looking for another route into composing for cash, Julyan stumbled into film music. A member of the UCL film society, where Nolan first cut his teeth directing, Julyan had joined not to become a director or cameraman, but just to make films. 'You would get a lot of people making bad films, including myself. Every now and again, you would get someone who made good films. When Chris came along, he wanted to crew his film properly; a lot of film-society projects were just a group of people who all wanted to be a director, and no one had written a script.'

Julyan had already worked with other society members when he teamed up with Nolan, who was determined to fashion a structured production method for his film-making. Collaborating on Nolan's shorts, *Larceny* and *Doodlebug* – 'trial runs', as Julyan calls them, 'to see if it was possible to make a finished film in that way' – the pair would again team up for *Following*, with Chris taking the unusual step of involving his composer from the early stages. It was an approach that they took into *Memento*, though 'not in a planned way', as Julyan notes.

An extra in *Following*, as well as a sound recordist on a couple of shooting days, Julyan spent most of his weekends at home in front of the keyboards, writing music, while the others were out filming. 'Because *Following* was shot every Saturday for months, we had a long time to allow the music to evolve,' he recalls. 'The music and the film informed each other. As Chris started getting a couple of rough-cuts of scenes together, I would look at those. He'd be doing rough-cuts, which I'd be doing music to, before other parts of the film had even been shot. It's odd to think how the music for *Following* evolved.'

It began with a piece of music taken from a collection of tracks Julyan had composed not specifically for *Following*. Even while writing the script, Nolan was listening to Julyan's music for inspiration, which, by default, became the main theme for the film. 'Chris always seems to have a sound in his head,' says Julyan. 'There'll be a couple of sounds that he'll be obsessed in getting, rather than melodies or tunes. With *Following*, there was a ticking noise that runs through the music, which he wanted. In *Memento* there are a lot of ominous rumblings.'

At this time, Julyan did not even have his trusty Mac – which, using a sequencing programme called Digital Performer, allows him to record CD quality tracks onto the computer's hard disk, before mixing everything digitally. 'Ten, or even five, years ago, I couldn't have produced the score in this manner,' he says. 'It's a nice way of working, because it means I can experiment with sound a lot more without worrying about paying for studio time.' Now, the only equipment he needed to hire, for completing the *Memento* score, was a digital multi-track machine, which allowed him to give Nolan the score in a form ready for a final polish on a professional sound stage.

Before Julyan embarked on *Memento*, his hardware consisted of an old Atari computer; as he calls it, 'the classic route of everyone starting out in music with no money'. With fewer keyboards, and no mixing desk, he had less flexibility, having to master his music from the computer straight to a DAT machine. It left less scope to mix the sound so subtly, though it still holds up. 'The biggest difference is in the way I wrote,' he says. Now able to lock his Mac in synch with the time-code on any video footage (to a frame-accurate degree) that he may be scoring, Julyan was once a practitioner in the fine art of improvisation – a skill essential for the sort of no-budget film-making that he and Nolan practised.

'On *Following*, partly because I didn't have the facilities, I used the rather primitive approach of pressing "record" at the same point every time. If we had a scene, I would always take my cue from the dialogue. Every time one of the characters said a certain word, I would press "record" on the Atari, and do that track. It can be done! In some ways, it seemed a shame to go from the eccentric method to the proper way.'

Julyan only upgraded days before he began work on *Memento* – though he believes his lack of experience with the equipment never actually compromised his work. Indeed, the end result, with its edgy, scratchy sounds jarring against deeply sad string sections, is testament to what can be achieved with a relatively small set-up. What is most remarkable, however, is the fact that Julyan composed the rough 'temp' tracks for the film before he purchased his Mac.

Nolan, unlike most directors, is not keen on using temp tracks – the dummy tunes placed on the soundtrack while the movie is being cut together. With most films, the composer is not usually invited to view the footage until the movie has been locked, and is nearing completion. Julyan cites his recent experience working on Michael Almereyda's *Happy Here and Now* (a gig won as a result of his work on *Memento*), where he arrived to find music from *The Limey* and *American Beauty* laid down to – temporarily – fit the mood of the film. As Chris explains, however, it's not a method he subscribes to.

'I don't like using temps because if it works, you get very attached to pieces of music and the combination of the image. If I was to send that to Dave [Julyan], I'd say, "We'll do it like this but different." To me it's not an ideal way of working. It's much better, if you can, to get some music that has been specifically crafted for your project, based on your script, or conversations or early footage.'

Julyan had read an early draft of the script to *Memento* back in the summer of 1998, a year before they would begin shooting, when he had gone to Los Angeles on holiday. By May the following year, he had read a revised version, and he and Nolan began exchanging ideas for the music. It was at this point that Chris asked his friend to pen some rough tracks for the film, adding, rather off-handedly, 'and we'll take it from there'. During the months of August and September, Julyan began composing, starting even before the shoot itself had commenced. It was his work here, back in London, that would form the basis for the score; a series of temp tracks, but ones written by the film's composer, and not merely music appropriated from another movie.

'We had discussed some ideas, like having a simple descending string theme, and something that was oppressive and rumbly,' says Julyan. 'I sat down and wrote six pieces of music, and sent them to Chris. From those six, the motel music – which was initially called "Oppressive Drone"! – is pretty much the same as the initial one I wrote. There was another one that I wrote that pretty much made it into the film as I wrote it, when he's in the motel room, tattooing himself. I think they even cut a scene to it.'

It's a method that ultimately seems rather indicative of the type of film-maker Nolan is; during early stages of the edit, or even the shoot itself, he was able to feel the mood of the film from Julyan's initial outpourings. And just as the film, with its subjective inserts, keeps us squarely inside Leonard's head, so Nolan was able to immerse himself further into the filmic experience by using tracks that would approximately resemble the final sound.

'I think I told him something along the lines of Nine Inch Nails meets John Barry,' laughs Nolan, in trying to recollect what sound he required Julyan to capture. Chris was also influenced, in his mind, by Terence Malick's *The Thin Red Line*, as he was for the filming of the flashback sequences. 'He really loved Hans Zimmer's score,' admits Julyan. 'And I do think it's one of Zimmer's best. It's very simple and very evocative. Chris had instructed me to go and see the film and buy the CD. Though at the same time he hadn't instructed me to rip off *The Thin Red Line*! If Chris had been using a temp score, he might well have used that.' Certainly, the 'wonderfully emotional and deceptively simple' nature, as Nolan calls it, of Zimmer's work was something he hoped Julyan would achieve for *Memento*.

'I felt in terms of the colour sequences, I was looking for a very direct emotional connection with what the character's feeling,' he says:

> Those kind of emotions aren't always understood by the character; one of the points about the character in this dilemma is he feels things without understanding the specific reason why. He just feels something. I wanted a type of music that didn't have to be specifically tuned necessarily to a narrative element; it could just come and go under a particular scene, and just push the mood one way or the other. The character can't remember why he feels a particular way, and often he misinterprets that, so I wanted the music to be able to support that ebb and flow.

Nolan's main concern was to reinforce the difference between the black-and-white (objective) sequences and the colour (subjective) segments. While the presence or absence of hue was a pretty good starting point for that, the use of music, built around these moments, was also employed to underline the division. The tracks used for the colour footage are composed on a grand scale, brooding and classical in their sound and structure. 'We needed an emotional element for the colour sequences,' reiterates Nolan, 'and I wanted something that was quite specific in terms of sentiment, memory and melancholy.' Julyan cites the film's main string theme as 'the closest to a romantic theme', used when he is burning her possessions. He, however, is reluctant to think of it as 'Leonard's theme'. 'I don't really think of *Memento* having themes for people. The whole film is about Leonard, so everything's Leonard's theme. I think it's more themes for his moods.'

By comparison, the black-and-white sequences would layer the 'oppressive and rumbly' noise underneath Leonard's motel-room narration. 'Most people don't even notice it,' Julyan concedes, though it's a noise that seems to speak of Leonard's inner turmoil, or of a fate that awaits him. Says Nolan: 'For the black-and-white sequences, I wanted something far more extreme. There were a lot of feedback noises he used. There's basically an idea of paranoia in those sequences.'

Take the 'Oppressive Drone' track, one, as Julyan mentioned earlier, that remained virtually the same from its rough composition to the final score. Used, in the black-and-white sections, as Leonard is gruesomely recording information on himself, Julyan played it for me, recalling a Nolan obsession:

On *Following* Chris was into this as well. He has this thing about a high-pitched tension sound. I need to find one for *Insomnia* now. In this case, we had this feedback, which was essentially me with a load of guitar effects pedals and levers, twisting the knobs on the mixing desk, just so it started feeding back to each other. Enough to make an interesting noise, but not to degenerate into uncontrollable chaos. Towards the end, as he gets more and more paranoid, wondering what's going on outside his hotel room, there's a very close sound happening.

Understandably, Nolan saw as essential the blending of these two distinct styles of music for the final sequence where the black-and-white segments meet the colour. 'It brings the two strands together. If you listen very carefully, in the last colour scenes, when Teddy is explaining what's going on, you're hearing some of the melody that has been used in the black-and-white scenes; it works on a subconscious level, bringing the two time-lines together.'

To some extent, Nolan already prepares us for this with his earlier use of the music for Sammy Jankis. Julyan calls it his own personal favourite: 'I really loved the sound and the subtlety of the atmosphere. There's lots of odd synthesizer stuff going on behind it.' Used almost exclusively with Sammy, it does leak into the colour sequence of Leonard burning his wife's possessions, hinting not only at the forthcoming structural shift but also Leonard's unhealthy association with Sammy's life.

Uncertain of what inspired him when writing the music – 'It's like asking me how I write music, to which the answer is "I don't know!"' – Julyan began his task by writing notes on the scenes from the film that most touched him, such as Leonard's 'How can I heal?' speech.

'Half the key scenes don't have any music on them in the final film!' he laughs. 'So much of *Memento* is about the mood. It's really a case of immersing yourself in the film, and watching it over and over. You have to become a bit blinkered, and a bit obsessive. It wasn't Method-composing, though. There was always the joke with *Following*, where I should start following people to see what comes to mind, but that was a little bit too dubious! I have to absorb the mood of the film.'

Working on most of the tracks while still in London, Julyan would receive Fed-Ex-ed packages containing VHS copies of various scenes; he would, in return, send over CDs of his compositions. Prior to this, though, he returned to Los Angeles, to sit for a week in front of the Avid and 'spot' the film, talking through with Chris what was required and selecting where the cues would be. The fact that his own rough template tracks were already there, accompanying the images, made Julyan's task that much simpler. 'It was a better starting point than having nothing on it, or someone else's tracks,' he says. Certain scenes – such as the chase with Dodd – were not, however, even touched until Julyan had the images in front of him.

'Having worked with Chris before, it wasn't that difficult. We trusted each other. To know what he wanted was the main thing. There are situations where people can ask for things, which are not actually what they want. I'm sure part of the job is interpreting what the director really wants, rather than what he's asking for.'

That said, a number of tracks Julyan intended for one sequence ended up being used by Nolan for another – for example, the music used for when Sammy's wife dies. 'That was a general mood piece. That was one of the cases where I presented Chris with a temp track, and said, "This is a sad mood for the film." He put it on the Sammy scene, and it could've been written for the film. It's an interesting part of the collaboration. If I write tracks for Chris, he sometimes does things with those tracks that were not intended.'

He had originally intended the repeated piano strain, used in the motel, as music to accompany Sammy. 'His scenes have this dated quality about them, where he sits there with this old TV and a big remote control,' says Julyan. 'Sammy is particularly out of time. Some of his stuff didn't seem to need music.' He cites, as an example, the music he penned for when Sammy is being tested with the electrified objects – ultimately used elsewhere in the film. 'It's quite a tension-building scene, but also a sad scene, because it's tragic as he doesn't know what's happening to him. That's why you have the repetitive piano, the weird feedback, but also the sad string bits coming in.'

As for the use of existing material, Nolan always knew he wanted to use a song at the end of the film:

> When you have such an abrupt ending, that leaves you in such a point of tension, I think you need a very active soundtrack over the credits, in order to release the tension for the audience. If it's too quiet, or silent, or we just reintroduce some of the quieter score, there's a strange feeling that you want the audience to diffuse. You want them to be able to relax, at the end of the film. Even though the narrative ending leaves you very tense, you want to be able to signal to the audience that the experience is over. It frees you up immediately to consider the film and start processing it in your mind.

Initially he thought of using Radiohead's 'Paranoid Android', which had been buzzing round his mind for some time. The opening track from the majestic *OK Computer* album, which Nolan had been listening to a lot while he was writing the script, it was an apt choice not only to conclude the movie, but to comment on Leonard's 'condition'. Nolan even used it in early private screenings, though, unfortunately, it proved too difficult to secure the rights to. The inclusion of the band's song 'Treefingers' on the soundtrack album to *Memento* offered some consolation to him.

Nolan, a huge Bowie fan, turned to his hero for help. With Bowie sharing the same agent – Chris Andrews – as Guy Pearce at ICM, a call was put in to try to secure 'Something In The Air', a track from *Hours*, Bowie's 1999 album released while *Memento* was in production. 'The song has some quite nice lyrical relevance, but more importantly than that, it was about the sound,' says Nolan. A melancholy song about the break-up of a relationship, Bowie's distinct vocals belt out lines like 'I guess you know I never wanted anyone more than you'. A veritable hymn to Leonard's loss, one verse in particular sums up the horror of his moment-to-moment existence:

> Lived all our best times
> Left with the worst
> I've danced with you too long
> Say what you will
> There's something in the air.

Nolan first heard the track when he and Aaron Ryder were driving up to Jennifer Todd's house for dinner one night in Ryder's car. After making contact with Chris Andrews, who was 'instrumental in securing the song', a copy of the script was sent to Bowie himself, though the film was not screened to him. 'Securing songs by an artist like David Bowie is never easy to do,' says Ryder, 'but in retrospect it wasn't that difficult. It wasn't that exorbitant.'

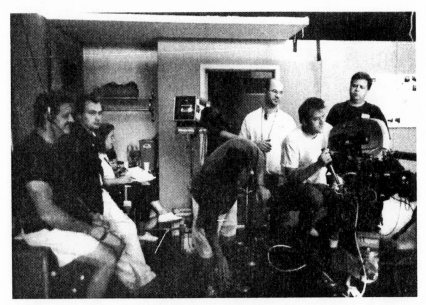

The crew of *Memento*.

DoP Wally Pfister, producer Emma Thomas, and Christopher Nolan.

Guy Pearce and Wally Pfister.

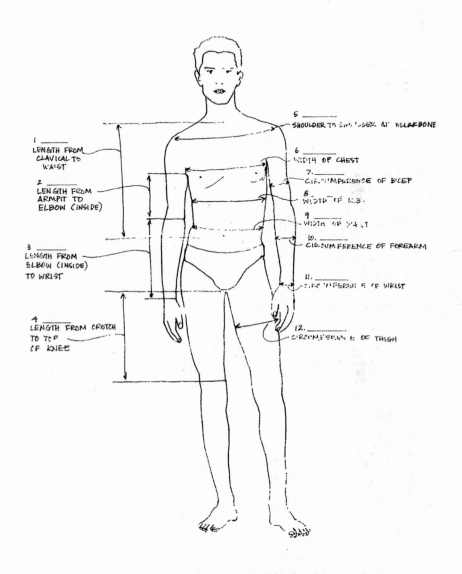

1 _____
LENGTH FROM
CLAVICAL TO
WAIST

2 _____
LENGTH FROM
ARMPIT TO
ELBOW (INSIDE)

3 _____
LENGTH FROM
ELBOW (INSIDE)
TO WRIST

4 _____
LENGTH FROM CROTCH
TO TOP
OF KNEE

5 _____
SHOULDER TO SHOULDER AT COLLARBONE

6 _____
WIDTH OF CHEST

7. _____
CIRCUMFERENCE OF BICEP

8 . _____
WIDTH OF RIB.

9 _____
WIDTH OF WAIST

10. _____
CIRCUMFERENCE OF FOREARM

11. _____
CIRCUMFERENCE OF WRIST

12. _____
CIRCUMFERENCE OF THIGH

Above: The body as canvas: a preliminary sketch by
production designer Patti Podesta.
Overleaf: A selection of sketches for Lennys tattoos by Patti Podesta.

103

THE FACTS:

LEARN BY REPETI[TION]

FACT 1: MALE

04277

PHOTOGRAP[H]
HOUSE
CAR
FRIEND
FOE

FACT 2. WHITE

I'M NO DIFFERENT

FACT 4.
LAST
NAME:
G____

FACT 3.
FIRST NAME
JOHN

PIN = 3853

[ERED M]

[A]

[RAPED]

[MURDERED MY WIFE]

MEMORY IS TREACHERY

find him and kill him

MY WIFE

AND MURD

JOHN G.

remember
Sammy Jankis

JOHN G. RAPED AND

Chapter 4

The casting

Time to take another step back in *Memento*'s production. The casting process began in earnest from an early stage. 'It's such a fascinating part of making movies,' says Jennifer Todd. 'How you come so close to making it in different variations with different people, and then when you see the film you can't imagine it with anyone else. Say, *The Wizard of Oz* with Shirley Temple!'

Or *Memento* with Brad Pitt. Early discussions for the casting of Leonard led to the heart-throb star. Aaron Ryder had a drink with one of Pitt's agents, John Levin, who was desperately looking for a vehicle for his client – 'a Sean Penn type of film', as Ryder puts it. 'I, of course, said, "*Memento* – that's the one." Pitt read it, and totally agreed. Chris met with Brad, and I thought we were going to be making a Brad Pitt movie. That would've been a much bigger film, and a bigger budget.'

Pitt passed, partially due to a schedule conflict – though Ryder's contact with the actor enabled him later to show Pitt the script for another of his babies, *The Mexican*. Released in 2001, with Pitt opposite Julia Roberts, it was a far more commercial vehicle than *Memento*, and more suited to his female fan-base. Yet, as Jennifer Todd remembers, he thought about *Memento* a great deal:

> He called, through his [other] agent Kevin Huvane, at CA. Kevin called me one afternoon, at 3 o'clock, to tell me Brad is passing. At 3.02, he called back saying, 'Don't pass yet, he's still thinking about it.' We waited a while, and then finally he passed again. From what I understand, he had just shot *Fight Club*, and it hadn't come out yet, and they were all worried about him doing too much dark material back-to-back. I loved that he wanted to do the movie; I think it was cool that he was responding so strongly to the material. I loved him in *Twelve Monkeys*. I think Chris was relieved, because of the baggage that comes with working with any movie star. The

budget would've been higher, and maybe Newmarket would've wanted to be involved because more would've been at stake. What kind of animal would the movie have then become? You're the director of the next Brad Pitt movie.

With Pitt out of the frame, it was collectively decided to eschew the pursuit of A-list stars and make the movie for less money by using an affordable quality actor. As Joe Pantoliano says: 'It was a movie not driven by star power. Guy Pearce is a great actor that the industry knows; while Carrie-Anne and I were in a film that grossed over a billion dollars worldwide – but we weren't openers, y'know what I mean? The reason why they hired us, was that we were the guys they could afford to hire. We all worked for way less than we normally get, and we all have a partnership and ownership in the movie.'

While Pearce wasn't an 'opener', his credentials as an actor weren't in dispute (coincidentally, a critic would later call him 'a Brad Pitt who knows how to act'). Born in Ely, Cambridgeshire, in England, Pearce, along with older sister Tracy, was relocated to Geelong in Australia when he was just three. Prior to beginning an international film career, Pearce was best known for playing do-gooder teacher Mike in popular soap *Neighbours*, but his staggering ability to sub-merge himself in a role soon saw him forge a name in Hollywood. 'I wonder whether, subconsciously, the reason why I've chosen such different roles is because I did the same thing for four years,' he says. 'That's probably ingrained. I get bored with myself, and how I look on screen. I enjoy the extremes, but I wonder if I'm going to run out of things to do.'

When I first interviewed Pearce, ironically it was just days before he was due to film *Memento*. Speaking from his LA hotel room, principally to discuss his role in Antonia Bird's *Ravenous*, the situation comically reflected Leonard's conversation with the anonymous caller. At the time, Pearce was without his wife, Kate, who had stayed in Australia for the duration of the shoot. 'I needed to be by myself so I went to LA alone,' he would say later. 'It was a short shoot and because we were so intensely focused I didn't spend time missing my wife.'

Two roles had commanded critical acclaim worldwide, and they couldn't have been more different. His outrageous turn as a bitchy drag queen in Stephan Elliott's *The Adventures of Priscilla, Queen of the Desert*, followed by his slimy, toe-stepping cop Ed Exley in Curtis

Hanson's sublime James Ellroy adaptation, *LA Confidential*, indicated just how diverse an actor he was. It was what drew Jennifer Todd to him:

> My sister Suzanne had been obsessed with him, after seeing *LA Confidential*. She said, 'I can't believe that's the guy from *Priscilla*!' I remember when her husband had never seen *Priscilla*; they were home, swapping the DVD's of *LA Confidential* and *Priscilla*, going back and forth, looking at him. He's such an amazing chameleon. His agent, Chris Andrews, was one of the first people who responded back to the script, saying that Guy would likely be interested. As the agents respond, you get a list in your mind. Guy was my first choice, because he was the one I was most confident would be likeable still. It was very important that he be reading for Leonard.

Others being considered at the time included Aaron Eckhart, who had yet to make *Erin Brockovich* but had played in two Neil LaBute movies, most memorably as misogynist Chad in office drama *In the Company of Men*. 'I liked Aaron,' says Todd. 'I think he's an amazingly talented actor, but I worried that he wouldn't be soft or likeable enough. He has this harsh exterior. We never offered it to him, so I don't know if he would've done it, though Chris did meet with him.'

Thomas Jane, who made his name in shark-attack movie *Deep Blue Sea*, and also featured opposite Gene Hackman and Morgan Freeman in *Under Suspicion*, had also read the script, but – filming abroad – was unable to get back and meet Chris in time. 'Thomas Jane was so funny,' laughs Todd. 'I saw him recently, and he said, "I wanted that part so badly!" He really campaigned for the part, and had read it, and had his agent call and call and call. Since we couldn't get him in a room with Chris, we never really considered him. But he was very sweet.'

It was Pearce, though, who impressed Nolan and Todd the most. By their first meeting, Nolan was convinced that Pearce was not only a nice guy, but passionate about the material. Pearce, on the other hand, was nervous. 'I was a bit paranoid when I met with him, because I went in there thinking, "There's so much about this that I don't yet fully comprehend."' His desire for winning the role even extended to putting in a personal call to Nolan, a move that rather touched the director. 'I was very struck by that. After we'd met, I wanted Guy to do it. But then, we entered into the business of agents, which as a director – and I assume as an actor – you're totally outside.'

Nolan was particularly taken with the lack of 'celebrity' that Pearce brought with him to the role:

> When you make a film like *Memento*, you want the audience to feel that whoever you cast is not just going to perform a star persona that they developed in other films; that they're actually going to create something completely new and unique. Leonard is written as an Everyman, but you're really looking to create a character that no one has ever really quite seen on film. And that's the kind of actor Guy is. He never really wants to repeat himself. Even in things like changing appearance he considers it his privilege and responsibility, as an actor, to give us something different.

For Pearce, though, who had heard many a tale of Hollywood actors gaining parts because of the boundless enthusiasm shown, it was a necessary action:

> Part of me thinks, What do you have to do to prove that you're enthusiastic, and why give the role to someone who's just enthusiastic? I kept wondering about that, and wondered if I was a bit lazy, and I thought I must call Chris personally and say, Honestly, I'm really keen on this. I'm always very keen to look at interesting scripts. Every now and again you get a script that is delightfully different and inspirational and then you'll take a look at the films the director's done and they're films you're not interested in, so you're caught in this situation where you've got a great script but you don't quite trust the hands it's to be placed in. In this case, I was practically jumping up and down in my seat.

Understandable, given the journey Leonard takes. Pearce was initially attracted to working on a script that dealt with notions of self-deception:

> I'm fascinated with the conflict that goes on in someone's mind, between what they know about themselves, and what they think they know about themselves, and then what they present to other people and what they present to themselves. Suddenly here was a character where all those elements were really heightened. He's doing this grotesque thing of telling himself things by tattooing himself, profusely denying certain elements of his emotional state. All these things that seem so linked are so separate, in different

compartments . . . it's really difficult for me to explain. It was just a reaction I got when I read it.

It also gave Pearce the chance to change his appearance again, this time with dyed-blond hair. 'It's what I imagined when I read it – partly because I hadn't done it before. Something I picked up in the script was heat. I imagined tan and blond and sweaty and messy and scruffy. Ironically, it suited the palate of the film and I knew it was a cream suit he wears.' Nolan remembers that Pearce would put calls in, suggesting he find some way – be it dyed hair, facial hair or whatever – to distinguish Leonard from his previous work. 'Eventually, we settled on the blond hair. It wasn't what I had in mind, originally. I hadn't thought about it that much. I was initially worried that if he dyed his hair it would look dyed, but then I realized it would probably look pretty good. Obviously, you can always tell that it has been dyed, but it fits in very nicely with Leonard. It's a visual detail, as with the tattoos, as with the scratches, that implies a history or a back-story to the character.'

Turning in a performance full of guile, it's to Pearce's credit that we're fully sympathetic with Leonard's plight, despite his deadly actions. Desperate, lonely, vengeful, angry, sardonic, sly, confused, disorientated, it's a comprehensive array of emotions for an actor to go through. Praise for his performance, as you might expect, is universal from his colleagues, as demonstrated by Mark Boone, Jr. 'I felt that Guy Pearce was the best thing about the movie. He is phenomenal in the movie. The creation of this character, there's a lot there for him. But he is the deal in the movie, the money shot!'

Nolan points out that Pearce's commitment was 'total' during the shoot, though he wasn't surprised. 'When you meet him it's very clear how seriously he takes what he does, without taking himself seriously, which is a huge point in his favour. But that's the way I am as a director. I don't see any point doing anything halfway; you just have to dive in and commit yourself totally.'

It was also Jennifer Todd that suggested Carrie-Anne Moss for the part of Natalie, having been obsessed by her since seeing her as the PVC-clad Trinity in *The Matrix*. 'I always thought she was cool. When I read the part of Natalie, I thought she'd be great for it. When we were discussing different actresses, she was definitely my favourite.' While actress Mary McCormack, last seen opposite Minnie Driver in Mel Smith's *High Heels and Lowlifes*, would campaign for the role, having read the script, Moss was always the favourite. The actress immediately responded to reading the script. 'The script was so fantastic. It was one of those scripts that you read, and as it was unfolding, it was like watching the movie. I kept wishing I was reading it with someone else at the same time. So I could go, "Oh my God, can you believe this?"'

For Moss, *Memento* was the second of three films made back-to-back, following mob comedy *The Crew* and preceding patchy sci-fi thriller *Red Planet*. 'I was working – in terms of hours – incredibly hard. And all the travelling, and I was like "Oh my God, how am I going to do this?" – doing three in a row,' she says. It also showed Moss's strong work ethic engendered by her mother, Barbara, who had encouraged her since her childhood to head for the stage. Named after the Hollies' 1967 hit *Carrie Anne*, the girl from Vancouver needed little persuasion. 'I've wanted to act since I was little. I did all the school plays, and I sang in the choir. I was that kind of kid.' She even toured Europe with her choir from the exclusive Magee Secondary School, before she headed to Toronto in 1985 to begin a lucrative modelling career that took her from Japan to Spain. There she won a role on CBS series *Dark Justice*, which eventually switched from Barcelona to Los Angeles, where she, ironically, starred in a short-lived show called *Matrix*.

But it was the role of Trinity that propelled her to worldwide stardom. Infinitely cooler than Lara Croft and sexier than all three of the revamped *Charlie's Angels* crew, Moss's Trinity kickstarted a rash of female action heroines. But it was Moss's vulnerable moments that persuaded Nolan she would be right for the devious, two-faced Natalie.

'I loved her in *The Matrix*,' he says:

This would be the first time we'd seen her since that film. In *The Matrix*, she has these two sides: a very guarded side, but also at specific points, there are moments when she was allowed to open up and be a bit softer, visually and vocally. To me, those were the two sides we needed for Natalie. As it is, she added an enormous amount to the role that wasn't on the page. She read the script and really seemed to get the character and what she could do with it. She related the film quite well to *The Matrix*, which was a conversation we had the first time I met her. The films, to me, are very different, but at this base level they both deal with this idea of 'Is it real? Can we trust the reality around us?'

As for the role of Teddy, it was Carrie-Anne Moss who had recommended Joe Pantoliano, her co-star from *The Matrix*. Both at the same agency at the time, the pair had become friends during the making of the Wachowski brothers' film, even subsequently appearing together in Michael Hurst's 1999 little-seen thriller *New Blood* – 'a very bad film', as Pantoliano puts it.

'Joey's in so many movies that make money, so he's this lucky charm,' says Jennifer Todd. Films like *The Fugitive*, *The Matrix* and even Warner Brothers' surprise recent hit *Cats and Dogs* all benefited from the Pantoliano touch. 'It was important to Chris, and to all of us, that Teddy had a sense of humour,' continues Todd. 'We knew we had to have an actor who could be funny, otherwise he'd be so menacing. I was so glad it was him.'

While Pantoliano was not the first actor considered (comedian Denis Leary was mentioned, though proved unavailable), he met with Nolan for coffee at the King's Road Coffee House. 'We had a really pleasant conversation,' recalls the actor. 'I called my agent Gleb Kliner, who's no longer an agent but has a dot.com company called Coffee Clubhouse – which I think is funny, because this is the kind of movie where'd you go to a coffee house to talk about it. I said I thought Chris was a nice guy, but that he wasn't gonna hire me.' Chris, sensed Pantoliano, was unsure whether to hire him because of the baggage the actor carried, citing Paul Brickman's *Risky Business*, which saw him play an aptly named scumbag Guido the Killer Pimp. 'Chris was concerned the audience would think that I was the bad guy from the minute I came through the door,' says Pantoliano. 'Gleb convinced him that that was exactly the reason that he needed to hire me.'

Certainly, the New Jersey-born veteran character actor was best known for playing the turn coat. Think of over-his-head gangster Ceasar in the Wachowski brothers' debut *Bound*, or the traitor Cypher from *The Matrix*. Yet he brings a wealth of depth to the role of Teddy, a man who alternates between 'love and pity', as Pantoliano puts it. Nolan soon realized that Joey Pants was a more subtle actor than his type-casting would necessarily reveal:

I watched *The Matrix* again after the film and I suddenly noticed that what he does in that film is entirely different in small ways. He's not obviously an actor who transforms himself across each role. He has that character-actor face, and people have associations with him, which I thought worked in our favour. The way he speaks, it was significantly different to what he was doing on the film. I think I underestimated the extent to which he was creating a persona; he's quite like that, in terms of his liveliness, but he's much more eloquent in a slower way in *The Matrix*. He has a deeper voice.

As for the second tier of actors, Suzanne and Jennifer Todd were present at every casting session. 'It was great when we were casting, because we found people really got the movie,' says Jennifer Todd. 'Some people came in and just auditioned, while others came in and said, "Wow, this is such a cool movie!" Stephen [Tobolowsky] was one of those people. He really got it. That was fun, because you're never sure if people are going to think you're crazy or not!'

Cast in the crucial role of Sammy Jankis, Tobolowsky offers a performance of distinct pathos and poignancy. 'Stephen Tobolowsky is so great,' agrees Todd. 'We were really happy that he wanted to do this film. He's such a strong character actor.' Dallas-born, Tobolowsky has been acting for the past two decades, with appearances over the last ten years in such diverse films as *The Grifters*, *Thelma and Louise*, *Basic Instinct* and *The Insider*. Typical of his work would be the bothersome insurance salesman Ned Ryerson in Harold Ramis's *Groundhog Day*, a film, like *Memento*, that fantasizes about the cyclical nature of time and one Nolan could not help but think on during casting:

I did, though not in terms of 'That would be a good thing to do.' I have seen him in so many movies. When he came to talk to us, he – more than any of the other people who came in to talk about that role – understood that Sammy is the backbone of the entire story. He explained exactly why, and explained the inherent metaphorical quality of the whole story. He'd really thought about the script, and connected with it. Sammy, basically, in the script has one line. So we were always looking for an actor with familiarity to the audience, who was prepared to take on this role with just one line. And he was happy to do that because he'd figured out that character was the backbone of the story.

For the role of motel clerk Burt, the artful Mark Boone, Jr was chosen. Born in Cincinnati, Ohio, the hefty-figured Boone, Jr began his career in theatre with fellow hopeful Steve Buscemi. The pair would later appear in Martin Scorsese's contribution to portmanteau movie *New York Stories*, before working together on both of Buscemi's directorial efforts, *Trees Lounge* and *Animal Factory*. Previously having worked with *Memento* DP Wally Pfister on TV film *The Sketch Artist*, Boone, Jr has also worked with likes the of Sam Raimi (*The Quick and the Dead*), David Fincher (*The Game* and *Se7en*) and on Nolan favourite *The Thin Red Line*. Aptly cast as the laconic Burt, Boone, Jr's air of bemusement and dry sense of humour work well for the film.

'I really liked Mark Boone, Jr's look and his attitude,' remembers Jennifer Todd, which is more than Boone, Jr himself can recall – not even sure, when I enquire, how he got the role. Shooting two other movies at the time, his look was a happy accident. 'I was making this movie called *The Beat Nicks*. That's why I had those tusks!' He does, however, recall just what he felt when he had read the script:

> I picked up the script and from the very first page, when I read it, I was like 'Fuck you! C'mon, really!' Then I read the second page, and I was like 'You gotta be kidding!' By page ten, I was literally going like 'Fuck You!' at the end of every page, because there was no way to figure this out. It was just more and more infuriating at every new page. I refused to flip backwards! I was so infuriated with the script, and myself, for continuing to read. Normally, I would've gone 'This is baloney!', and not wasted my time. But I found myself pushing through this script, and I'd never experienced something like that before.

Larry Holden was cast as Natalie's boyfriend, Jimmy. Irish-born but American-based, Holden's task of shaping the character across one scene was tricky, and yet – with a pitch-perfect Stateside accent – he conveys what he has to: a cocksure swagger soon lost, colour draining from cheeks as he realizes the full extent of Leonard's intent. Holden, though, is tough on himself:

> I feel like I let Chris down in *Memento*. I went for some easy choices. At least in the beginning of that scene. And I told him and Emma that right after I saw it for the very first time. I'm extremely honest with myself, and I know I could've brought more to the table, and I didn't. I just said, 'Okay. Let's see . . . a drug dealer who gets killed and stripped down to his boxers . . . well, I better go to the gym and lose some fucking weight.' I talked to Guy about it not long

ago, and told him how I felt and that I was sorry, but he just gave me that sly, little smile of his and said, 'Aw . . . Larry, Larry, Larry.'

A writer-director himself, his own production ethic could easily be borrowed from Nolan. After shooting his Maryland-set debut *My Father's House* for $75,000, his second effort, the Cassavetes-inspired *A Foreign Window* was shot on digital video with, as he says, 'minimal crew, no make-up or wardrobe department, no fucking trailers, no whining, little actors'. A kindred spirit aside, he remains unsure as to why Nolan hired him:

> I think he liked the shape of my moustache that day . . . Seriously, though, I don't know what he saw in me. He and Emma were there – which I thought was cool, ya know, that they weren't just gonna have a tape of my audition sent to them somewhere; that they wanted to see it with their own fucking eyes – and they were friendly and all, but pretty much cool, calm, and collected. As usual. I finished, and looked straight at the casting director, John Papsidera, a prince in this town full of Palookas, who was also running the camera, and he snuck me a little thumbs-up sign on the sly.

Interestingly, Nolan specified the actor playing Jimmy must have facial hair, just as he did for Teddy and his 'sinister moustache'. Nolan explains the obsession: 'To me facial hair always comes across in these film characters as implying a certain amount of disguise. Watching the film again, and what Joey did with this character, it really is all about the spiky hair, the moustache and the glasses in front of this person. It's only really in the last scene that you start to see his eyes behind it. It's almost cartoonish, a distraction the character has. It definitely made him harder to read.'

As for Jimmy, the 'tache was there more as a memory trigger for the audience to relate back to the photograph we have briefly glimpsed of him and Natalie together. 'Actually, we tried a few different looks,' recalls Holden. 'Goatee, I think, a soul patch. Then we settled on Chris's original choice: the infamous "'tache à la Holden"! It drives Scandinavian women wild, ya know?' Given that Holden makes an appearance in Nolan's third film, the remake of Norwegian film *Insomnia*, it's just as well.

To play Dodd, Canadian-raised actor Callum Keith Rennie was cast.

Recently featuring in a number of key films from Canada (David Cronenberg's *eXistenZ*, Don McKellar's *Last Night*, Lynne Stopkewich's *Suspicious Rover*), Rennie had once before played a drug dealer, in John Dahl's *Unforgettable*. 'Callum just gave a great audition,' says Nolan. 'He really made something of the little scene we had him do, being found in the closet. He had the right look, as well. We didn't want to go with anybody who looked too obviously like a heavy. We shot him, though, to look more imposing.'

Rounding out the cast were *The West Wing*'s Jorja Fox, as Leonard's wife; Broadway star and *Frasier* actress, Harriet Sansom Harris, as Mrs Jankis – 'this little gem in the movie', as costume designer Cindy Evans notes; *3rd Rock From The Sun*'s Marianne Muellerleile as the tattooist; newcomer Kimberley Campbell as the blonde escort; Thomas Lennon as the doctor and even location manager Russ Fega, making a turn as the waiter.

The photography

January 1999. Chris Nolan's *Following* was at the Slamdance festival, the younger, more spirited brother of Robert Redford's Sundance jamboree. While there, he saw Ron Judkins' *The Hi-Line*, an adoption drama which starred Rachael Leigh Cook as a naive youngster who discovers her real mother is a Blackfoot Indian, living in the 'Hi-Line', a desolate area of Montana. Nolan was impressed by the film's naturalistic style, replete with stark, carefully composed shots, filmed in the dead of winter in Montana by one Wally Pfister, who would later win the Santa Monica film festival's award for Best Cinematography for the film.

'I knew it had been shot very efficiently and cheaply, but Wally had still managed to pull off some really beautiful imagery,' says Nolan:

I was always of a mind to try and find a DP who could work very efficiently, the same way I liked to work, because I knew we had to shoot fast but I still wanted to have a stylish look to the piece. Obviously, the fact that he shot a low-budget film that looked as good as it did was in his favour. What was really impressive was that he had tremendous restraint, which most photographers don't. There's an important scene in the film where a young girl meets her mother for the first time, and he does a slow dolly in on the protagonist, and he does it so slowly you wouldn't know it was there. I had to watch the shot on fast-forward on video to make sure it was a dolly, and not a zoom. It's so slow, you feel it rather than see it. That kind of restraint and subtlety is rare.

Sold at the festival by Next Wave films, who had provided finishing funds for Nolan's *Following*, *The Hi-Line* offered Chris an easy introduction to Pfister; advised by Next Wave chief Peter Broderick to hook up, the pair in fact missed each other in Park City, but it was clear that they shared certain sensibilities. 'I found later on that we had very similar tastes in photography,' says Pfister, 'and so I think he just responded to that.'

Pfister did not in fact see *Following* until after he was hired on *Memento*. Working on a low-budget feature called *Rustin* in Alabama, he was sent the script by his agent. Working a six-day week, Wednesday to Monday, Pfister read it on his day off, and was blown away. 'Of course, I had to read it again,' he says:

I immediately responded to my agent, saying I was dying to do the movie. My agent said the only way that it would happen was if I was able to meet with Chris. And there I was, on the other side of the country, working six days a week. We finished shooting, at night, on a Monday. We wrapped at 4 a.m. I stayed up, and took a 7.30 a.m. flight, having worked the entire night before, flew into LA, met with Chris at noon that day for about an hour, went back to the airport – without even going to my home – and had to wait for about three hours, before catching a late-afternoon flight back to Alabama. I then went to the set and shot an entire day's worth. I was up for a solid three days. I credit my agent for really pushing me to do it. But it was that important to me. I knew it was a gem of a script – a once-in-a-lifetime opportunity.'

During that first meeting, Pfister admits that he wasn't sure if he had formulated a full understanding of the material. Subsequently reading the script five times, Pfister was initially impressed by the screenplay's intricate structure, but it was a connection to the material on a more personal level that struck him like a freight train:

My father had a bit of a short-term memory problem. To this day, it's still difficult for me to see some of the scenes with Sammy Jankis. Although those situations are somewhat extreme exaggerations of what my father's condition is – he's 72 years old and it's more common at that age – at that time, when the script came to me, my whole family was beginning to struggle with that. So it had an incredible personal connection. I mentioned that in my first meeting with Chris. I told him that it had an emotional grip over me. I'm never able to look at those scenes objectively, in terms of how that manipulates an audience because I always have a personal response. I've always wondered if everybody has the same sort of feelings, or whether its motivated by my own life situation.'

Once on board, Pfister and Nolan began discussions about capturing the look for *Memento*. Strangely, the one film-maker that didn't come up in discussions was Nicolas Roeg, a natural father-figure for Nolan in terms of both form and content, and a big influence on Pfister. 'I've always been an enormous fan of Nic Roeg,' he says:

Even some of his more obscure films, like *Track 29*; but *Don't Look Now* is just an incredible, haunting film. We never talked about that film, but it really came up later on in discussion. The way that film is photographed – it's shot in that Seventies style – very naturalistic, no bullshit. Before this whole hyper-stylized photography. It's right in line with some of my favourite cinematography from that era; people like Gordon Willis, Néstor Almendros, Vittorio Storaro. If you revisit *Apocalypse Now*, that's the work I really love. It was a wonderful source of inspiration for me.

New York-born, Pfister began his career in Washington, DC, as a member of the press corps covering the White House, State Department and Capitol Hill. Later, his focus on documentary work earned him two Emmy awards for the acclaimed PBS series *Frontline*. Moving to Los Angeles in 1988, he attended a cinematography program at the AFI, where he photographed the Academy Award-nominated short film *Sen-Zeni-na* and met Steven Spielberg's now-regular DP Janusz Kaminski. Employed at Roger Corman's legendary Concorde production company in 1991, where Kaminski also worked, Pfister worked as a second-unit DP for a year, including on the horror film *The Unborn*. Not surprisingly, it was here he learnt to set up and shoot quickly, a skill Nolan would welcome for the *Memento* production. There he met cinematographer Phedon Papamichael, and would subsequently serve as his camera operator for nine years.

Working with him on a number of high-profile projects, be they Hollywood (*Mouse Hunt, Stuart Little, Phenomenon, While You*

Were Sleeping) or art-house (*Million Dollar Hotel, Unstrung Heroes, Tanner '88*), Pfister went on to lens a series of best-forgotten low-budget sequels, such as *Animal Instincts II* and *Amityville: A New Generation*.

As it happened, this experience was something else that attracted Nolan to employing Pfister:

> I was looking for a DP who could operate the camera himself, so that I could remove a layer of communication that I was having to take on. In *Following*, I shot the film myself, so I was very worried about inserting an extra two people in the process; if you could make it one, that would be better. And it was. We had a directness of communication that was very valuable. It simplified the process a lot. I'm a good operator, myself. I enjoy it a lot. I was very worried about not being able to do that on a bigger film, because I didn't have the experience.

The chance to shoot *Memento*, however, offered Pfister the opportunity to work on a serious-minded project, and stamp his style – 'clarity and realism' – across it. 'Realism is what I'd have to say is my style, as a cinematographer,' he says. 'It's the only photography I can understand. I can't do a stylized music-video look. I have to base my work in reality, and that's the kind of storytelling I like to do. I think that really is the essence of it.'

Nolan had already come into the film with the notion that he wanted to shoot in anamorphic, a format Pfister himself preferred to Super 35, and one traditionally used for capturing vast vistas and landscapes, as seen in the works of, say, John Ford or David Lean. 'I was very excited [that] he had made the decision to shoot in anamorphic before I came on board,' says Pfister:

> He mentioned it to me in the initial meeting. I love that aspect ratio. It mocks human eyesight better. You get the peripheral vision in there. It's a great way to get inside a character. Here it works really well, because by opening up the sides, you can put the character in frame, and have some of the elements of what you see in the frame as well. It worked well from that perspective. What Chris liked about it was that with anamorphic, you have less depth of field. It means that less is in focus. So if you're focused clearly on Guy's face, for example, the background would

be less in focus than if you were shooting the other way – and Chris loved that notion. You could really focus on the character.

Whereas widescreen's aspect ratio is 1.85:1 – meaning a smaller area of the negative is used, ultimately offering a grainier picture quality – anamorphic (aspect ratio: 2.35:1) provides a crisper image. 'It's not usually applied to interior, claustrophobic stories,' says Nolan. 'But I felt that, in taking on Leonard's world, that is this immediate space around him, and treating that with a format usually used for land-scapes, we would actually exaggerate the feeling of claustrophobia.'

Nolan, in fact, wanted Pfister to look at two films by Adrian Lyne, a surprising choice given the gross excess of some of his better-known works, such as *Flashdance* and *9½ Weeks*. Two of Lyne's better films, his 1998 nostalgia-tinged remake of *Lolita* and his nightmarish 1990 Vietnam-conspiracy film *Jacob's Ladder*, were screened, for their – as Pfister puts it – 'fairly natural, non-pretentious lighting'. Both were scrutinized for the way Lyne uses inserts (close-up shots indicating a direct point of view), something Nolan was very keen to get right, as part of his means of keeping the audience within Leonard's world:

> Chris showed me the film [*Lolita*], and how they used them in a fashion that was the natural part of the story-telling, rather than what I had done for many years as a cinematographer and as an operator, which was to shoot inserts to drive home a point. I think they have been mis-used so often in film. Chris's point was really to integrate them in a natural way. And what happens that way, once you're used to it, is that they become little snippets of Leonard's memory. It was the most effective use of inserts I have ever seen. [With *Jacob's Ladder*] I was able to dial into the way the inserts were shot. I don't know if you remember the trolley going down the hallway, but there's an insert of the wheel going back and forth over this piece of flesh. It's in a very natural light. Jeff Kimball shot that movie, and I think he's a very talented, and somewhat under-rated, cinematographer, and I thought he did a spectacular job.

During the shoot, the inserts were shot by the first-unit camera crew, a task Chris was insistent was left to them, and not the second or clean-up unit. 'Quite often, the second-unit insert shots need to be re-shot, or there are continuity problems. It does make sense to have the first unit do them wherever possible,' says Pfister. 'Chris was adamant, and it took a bit of pushing against the first AD [Assistant Director] and the production manager. He constantly had to repeat to the first AD, "If we don't get it now, they'll never get shot." That was really the driving fear; that somebody might say to him "We can't afford a second unit," or "We don't have time." His thinking was to get them while he could.' It meant shooting the inserts from any particular scene immediately after the main action was captured, before the next set-up was approached. 'I would start lighting with that in mind. I would keep the area where we did the inserts lit at the same time as lighting the entire scene, so we could jump right into it.' Pfister would often simply grab his camera, hand-held, and get the inserts in the can. Rather than using a double, Guy Pearce insisted on doing all of the insert work himself.

'Chris was thrilled about that,' confirms Pfister. 'It's a little unusual for the actor to do that much. Guy definitely went above and beyond what would be expected of an actor. He did stuff only he could do, in order to match properly. In addition, he did stuff that anyone could've done. In contrast, in the film we completed with Al Pacino [*Insomnia*], quite a bit of the insert work was done with Al's double.'

Another, more recent film, Terence Malick's *The Thin Red Line*, was also – as it would be on David Julyan's score – very influential on *Memento*'s cinematography. 'Malick's movie had a pacing and a feel to it that was very real, a combination of all the elements – performance, sound design, music, cinematography – coming together to create a mood,' says Pfister. Shot by John Toll, Malick's 1999 adaptation of James Jones's novel, a mournful hymn to the World War II Battle of Guadalcanal and a meditation upon nature, beauty, love and death, indeed harks back to the work of the esteemed cinematographers from the Seventies that so impressed Pfister.

Pfister and Nolan specifically looked at Malick's use of flashbacks in the film, in connection to the scenes where Ben Chaplin's Private Bell thinks about his fickle wife. Filmed almost like a home movie, in a haze of summer colours, the clips were highly distinct from the rest of the movie. 'What Chris really liked about the way the flashbacks worked in that picture was that there was no fan fare,' says Pfister. 'They weren't slow-motion, or done in sepia tones. They weren't in your face; also there wasn't any grand sound design change. They just popped up very naturally, like little snippets of someone's memory. That was the template, the starting point, for those sequences.'

Nolan had already decided, before seeing Malick's film, that he wanted his flashbacks to cut in with 'no trickery'. He was also taken with Malick's use of 'very tactile images of memory', evocative and personal triggers. 'I felt that when you try to remember somebody from the past, all you are left with is these small things. When I saw that film, I was very stuck by it. Then I had to decide whether to do it that way, or try and come up with something different. In the end, I felt the only honest way to cut those images in was the way Terence Malick had done it: to just cut it in. If you cut it in in the right place, you don't need any dissolves.'

For the black-and-white sequences, Nolan was looking for a distinct separation between the scenes of Leonard in the motel room and the Sammy Jankis story. Chris initially proposed using a hand-held *cinéma verité* style, with the camera's frequent movement differentiating the scenes from the more static colour segments. Although, ultimately, the camera is less volatile than was first suggested, the sequences manage to convey a pseudo-documentary feel, undoubtedly testament to Pfister's own work for PBS.

'In the black-and-white sequences, we wanted to have more of this style,' confirms Nolan. 'We felt able to then move the camera off his eye-line, higher or lower. So when he goes to the sink, we're beneath his waist looking up at him. When he sits on the bed at the end, when he sees the "Never Answer The Phone" tattoo, you really get that sense of a rat-in-a-box, by pulling wide and showing him in that way.' After the tightly held close-ups of Leonard, these disconcerting wide-angled shots Nolan refers to visually trigger the idea that we should be looking at the protagonist in a more objective way. Along with the black-and-white footage implicitly suggesting this objective, artificial view-point, the camera's blocking (or placement), in fact, was planned to emphasize the same point, partly by Chris's refusal to pull so-called 'wild-walls'. The fourth wall of a set, it can normally be removed to permit access for the camera equipment and crew: Chris kept things cramped, deliberately.

'That's pretty unusual if you're on a set, because on set you generally pull a wall just to get access to a camera, and have some breathing room, or to move the camera back,' says Pfister. 'Chris had a great philosophy, which was a new approach to me, and I have taken it with me since. This was, that the camera should never be someplace where it can't be. If you built a set, and you establish the set – the walls are, say, 12 x 15. Anytime you pull that camera back beyond 15 feet, which

122

you can do by pulling the so-called wild-wall on the set, then you are going outside of where that camera belongs in the room.'

While Chris would pull walls to allow the crew to get some air, they generally remained faithful to this dictate, one that Nolan himself had found others roundly rejected:

I feel very strongly, and a lot of DPs I've talked to disagree, that the audience is always aware of where the camera is, aware of the perspective and point-of-view they're seeing, in terms of camera blocking. So this blocking is very important to me. Therefore, I am not happy to choose a frame that needs a zoom lens. If you want the camera closer to the action, you need to move the camera closer. The frame size to me is a different thing. A lot of cinematographers and directors view the frame size as the thing; I don't. I view the camera as the thing. If you pull a wall, and you take the camera back 30 feet, and use a zoom lens, to put a tight shot on the actors, I believe the audience is aware on some level that it isn't the same and that they feel you're outside that space. That can have an interesting effect, but I didn't want to make the sets feel artificial.

As far as the lighting was concerned, Chris felt it was important to keep a single, strong light source in the back of viewers' minds. It came from the window, which was covered by both a shield and a pair of curtains:

I felt if we could create a strong, directional light, which would give these great shadows, it would give it a very *noir*-ish feeling. And also create that kind of directional lighting [you get] when you move around the subject and you shoot the subject from different sides for different scenes. You actually achieve a completely different effect then, using, realistically, the same lighting, so that when you shoot from the window side, it's relatively flat. When you shoot towards the window, it's almost completely a silhouette. Broadly speaking, we started shooting towards the window, and then moved around half-way, and then at the end, there are some shots looking back into the room. It's all in that *noir*-ish shadowy style, and there's something about the way we shot those scenes that makes them distinct from the other ones.

By contrast, the lighting for the Sammy Jankis segments was designed with a different aim in mind. Says Pfister: 'The Sammy Jankis stuff has a different texture to the black-and-white; it's a brighter, flatter light. The stuff within the hotel room is definitely a darker, more contrasting light.' Meanwhile, the camera's blocking – for a story, of course, being retold by Shelby – was more traditional, using a dolly and tripod to increase the stability. Curiously, Pfister – who operated the camera himself throughout the entire shooting of the colour sequences and the black-and-white motel scenes – asked his assistant Bob Hall – 'for my money, the best focus puller in Hollywood' – to operate here. 'It was so I could look at the take in black-and-white on the monitor. We don't often use the monitor, but that was an area where I didn't want to look through the camera. I had Bob do a lot of the black-and-white work; not the hand-held stuff, I did that.'

Nolan himself would use the monitor as a 'tool', as Pfister puts it. During the production, mounted on the camera was an on-board monitor, usually used to see if the picture is in focus. 'Chris would glance back and forth between the small monitor and the actors. He spent a lot of time right next to camera. Often, I would float with the camera, and I would do a documentary style, going off on my own to get the pieces I knew Chris wanted. But for performance, he would sit next to the camera and watch the actors.'

Working with a Panavision Gold II camera, for the colour work, Pfister used a slower speed film to keep the grain structure strong. The interior colour sequences, of course, were to be expressing Leonard's point of view subjectively, the camera forever in his face. But, knowing that colour and black-and-white will intertwine in the film's last act, Nolan prepares us for this twist, with the camera's blocking. Just as he would with the score (mingling cues from both the colour and black-and-white segments towards the close of the film), so he uses the camera to suggest this structural union. As an example, Nolan cites the scene when Leonard is sitting on Natalie's couch, with her asking him why the police have yet to catch the intruder. 'During that sequence, the camera leaves Leonard's point of view and moves up to hers. To me that was very important in terms of bringing the colour and the black-and-white together. That really suggested for the first time that the audience should look at Leonard more objectively. I think it instantly changes your perspective on him, and what you've accepted.'

While most of the colour sequences were filmed inside, a certain amount was shot out-of-doors. Chris specified to Pfister that, in an ideal world, the day shots would be overcast, to help the 'grim portrayal of the environment', as the DP terms it. 'I'd originally envisaged shooting further north, and getting gloomier weather,' says Nolan. 'The advantage of California is that the weather is always great, so you always shoot. But this makes it difficult in terms of the fact that the sky has a very harsh light, a deserty sun.' A technical nightmare at the back end of a long, hot summer, Pfister set about devising a shooting schedule with first AD Christopher Pappas where, whenever possible, the scenes were not shot in direct sunlight so a softer light could be found. Or, if they were, it would be used as a back-light, in a way that didn't stand out.

'We were able to do that quite a bit of the time; for instance, finding the best time of day, say, at the motel,' says Pfister. 'Basically, Chris was very supportive of the schedule I proposed, in terms of shooting the motel after 2 p.m. because the sun goes the other side, and this side is in shade after 4 p.m. – and vice versa. It's very difficult to do on a 25 day shooting schedule, but sometimes we were able to do it, and other times we weren't.'

The shoot

Shot on a remarkably tight schedule – officially from Tuesday, 7 September to Friday, 8 October 1999 – Nolan needed to be on full alert to get *Memento* in the can. What follows is a day-by-day breakdown of what was shot, with – where appropriate – cast and crew recollections of that day. But first, Wally Pfister, on how Nolan managed to command the respect of his production crew:

> Chris has an incredible political sense of dealing with the powers
> that be, the production managers or the producers. He is able to
> really communicate to them and make it clear to them what he
> absolutely needs. Where they tell him it can't be afforded, he'll
> work with them. He really is a master at working the system too. He
> really is a producer himself. He has those negotiating skills, and has
> control of the set in that respect. He kind of ADs his own set. He's
> really capable of a number of things at once. The crew loved him, in
> both cases on both films [*Memento* and *Insomnia*]. Often you'll see
> a crew turn on the director if he's not showing them respect; you'll
> get directors who won't even say "Hi" to them. But pretty much
> everyone on the crew liked and respected Chris. At a certain point,

a VHS copy of *Following* was passed around among the crew, and they were very impressed.

Only Jonah, as the younger brother, got snubbed: 'I exchanged about five or six words with him, while we were working on the film. I think at one point he got on the radio, and told me to clean up some shit that was on the steps of his trailer. But we had the usual antagonistic older–younger brother situation, which was entirely comfortable because it was his film and I was just along for the ride. When he's making a film, he's particularly single-minded.'

Day 1: The only day all three principal cast members were on set, the scenes shot were exterior sequences outside of Natalie's house. The first scene was Teddy warning Leonard about Natalie; the second saw a freshly bruised Natalie sit in her car and then get out; the third was Leonard and Natalie pulling up to the house.

Day 2: The interior bedroom scenes at Natalie's house, calling for Pearce and Moss to be on set. Scenes shot were Leonard waking up beside Natalie at daybreak, and then three night scenes – Leonard delivering his 'How can I heal?' speech; Natalie waking to find Leonard's side of the bed empty; and Leonard returning to bed.

Moss came well prepared, having taken her script apart and put it in sequence. She also removed her scenes and re-ordered them chronologically, an idea that partly came from her and partly from her acting teacher. 'She [the teacher] was very confused by it and she re-arranged it, and I wanted to do it. Christopher had said 'Don't do it' because I think he was afraid that if somebody got their hands on what was a more conventional story, they might turn it around, or might not think that it worked, whatever. But I did take it apart, and I worked on that sequence to find my character.'

Pearce, of course, had the same dilemma:

It was definitely a situation for me where I really had to try and understand what Chris's intention was, which was not necessarily about finding the answers to the questions – it was about the question itself. I had to go through a number of stages of rationally and logically working out what I needed to work out, and then get rid of that. Pulling the script apart, for example, and looking at the script in a linear sense just so that I could understand the continuity of emotions. But then putting it away because of the condition that Leonard is suffering from. It was much more unusual than most films I've worked on.

Day 3: Again calling for Pearce and Moss, two scenes inside Natalie's apartment – this time in the living room – were shot. Natalie setting Leonard onto Dodd was followed by the scene where Leonard tells her about his wife's murder.

Day 4: Remaining with the same two cast members, and in the same location, the moment Leonard hits Natalie was shot, as well as his dusk-set approach to her door, where he quizzes her about Dodd. Referring to the expletive-ridden rant she delivers to Leonard, Moss glows with pride: 'That was a real fun scene to shoot, and indicative of how very liberating the movie was to make. There was a lot of creative freedom within it, because of the way the story was told.'

Day 5: Three night scenes, again in Natalie's living room, were shot: Natalie offering to help Leonard; the sequence where Leonard studies the photo of Natalie and Jimmy; and Leonard writing on the Polaroid snap of Natalie.

Day 6: This saw a move to Ferdy's Bar – aka The Blue Room in Burbank – first for the exterior scene where Leonard pulls up in the Jaguar and enters the bar; inside, two more scenes were shot, with the need for a number of extras, including a drunk, described as a 'grubby male'! The first of the two saw Natalie bring Leonard the spit-ridden beer tankard, then take it away; the second, at dusk, saw Leonard, 'the memory guy', talk to Natalie.

A day scene, it gave Wally Pfister the chance to mix daylight – from the bright window in the background – with some warm tungsten lights inside. He also got production designer Patti Podesta to place lamps – with a contrasting cobalt blue base – around the bar (they can be glimpsed behind Leonard in the shot of him in the booth). 'All the walls were blue, so I kept the light warm on them. We had this great contrast going – that's what I think you see and what leaps off the screen, which is the contrast between this cobalt blue and the warm flesh tones.'

Day 7: The restaurant scenes were next, concluding Moss's stint on the film. The first sequence that day was the waiter giving Leonard his envelope; the second, was Natalie doing the same; the third was an exterior shot of Leonard arriving at the building, and finally – on what was a lengthy day – Leonard in the washroom, discovering the 'Remember Sammy Jankis' tattoo.

Day 8: The first of the black-and-white scenes were shot – with Leonard in his office, dressed in his 'cheap, dark suit', as the schedule notes, talking on the phone about how people lie. The second scene was with Harriet Sansom Harris, as Mrs Jankis arrives wanting to know the truth about Sammy's condition. We then switched to the nursing home, for the shot of Sammy watching people. Aside from heralding the arrival of Stephen Tobolowsky on set, Guy Pearce, of course, was also required for this sequence, as Nolan fractionally cuts from Sammy to Leonard. The two medical scenes were then completed: Sammy failing his test over and again, followed by the doctor examining his patient.

Day 9: The crew then set off to the suburbs near Pasadena, for the Jankis household. First scene was Sammy watching TV and injecting his wife with insulin. The scene where Leonard arrives at the front door to notice a notch of recognition in Sammy's face was then completed. Following this, the confrontation between Sammy and his wife was shot. The final scene of the day called – mysteriously – for the presence of Guy Pearce and Jorja Fox, despite it being the moment when Sammy injects his wife with insulin repeatedly until she dies. In fact, it was never an intention of Nolan's to put subliminal flashes of Lenny and his overdosing wife into the scene. Both actors were simply on call in case Nolan wanted to shoot their corresponding 'injection' scene.

Day 10: A switch to Leonard's apartment, calling for Pearce and Fox to be on set. Some seven colour-stock scenes were shot on this day. In order, the day scenes were: Leonard recalling his wife; Leonard's wife smiling; Leonard's wife being injected with a syringe and being pinched; then at night, in the bedroom, Leonard talking to his wife about the book she's reading; Leonard noticing his wife is missing, and finally, Leonard retrieving his gun, going into the corridor and then down the hallway.

Day 11: This saw the return to the set of Joe Pantoliano, who had so far only done one day's work on the film, as well as the first day for

Callum Keith Rennie. Moving to the exterior of Dodd's motel room, three sequences were shot: Leonard's fish-eye view of Teddy; Leonard knocking the wrong guy out at the door; the kidnapping of Dodd. Later on, the crew headed to Burbank-located diner The Grinder for the discussion of memory held between Teddy and Leonard.

Pearce recalls being excited at the chance to work with Joey Pants:

He has such a lively energy. It really helped in determining the place that Leonard can cocoon himself into. Joey would be buzzing around like a crazy man, and I suppose it was like the way some animals react to other animals when they're being attacked – they'll sit still and just observe, and so would I. Joey brought such a great energy. We were talking about this the other day; whether that energy is Joey or the character. I'm sure Joey's personality changed while he was doing the role. There was a quality about Joey that was almost absent-minded, which gave me cause to just observe where he was coming from, and wondered whether I would believe that we knew what he was up to as a person, via the character.

Day 12: A number of action shots were captured on this day. Firstly, Leonard driving away from the tattoo parlour, followed by his drop from the window. The screech to a halt outside the building was then shot, before moving on to the trailer park. The chase between Leonard and Dodd and then Dodd's enquiry about the Jaguar car were shot, before moving to the sequence where Dodd pulls Leonard over.

Day 13: A remarkable number of scenes were shot on this day, all at the Discount Inn in Tujunga. Day exterior shots first: Leonard entering the motel's office; Teddy and Leonard walking to the car park; three separate scenes where Leonard heads to the motel office; Leonard heading to room 304, then arriving at it. With the arrival on set of Mark Boone, Jr, the scenes where Burt unlocks room 21 and Leonard discovers that he's been renting two rooms were also completed. Two black-and-white sequences were also shot: outside the Discount Inn, the moment when Teddy gives directions to the derelict house; and the phone call Leonard takes from Burt in room 21.

Day 14: More Discount Inn scenes in the can: the blonde arriving at room 304; Leonard telling Burt, at the office, he has lost his key; Leonard meeting Teddy in the office; Leonard talking to Burt as Teddy arrives. Outside, three car sections were shot: Leonard, by day, stepping into the Jaguar; and at night, Leonard heading to the car and leaving the motel behind the wheel.

Day 15: A trip to the derelict building in Carson, Long Beach, for two of the film's earliest scenes, where Teddy and Leonard arrive, was followed by the film's later sequence where Jimmy – and then Teddy – pull up. The scene where Leonard emerges, requesting help from Teddy, was also shot, as was the moment where Leonard opens the trunk of the car, preparing to steal it. By nightfall, the crew moved to the nearby refinery to film Leonard burning his wife's things, as well as completing the shot of Leonard kicking out the embers of the fire he's created.

Shot in the San Pedro area of California, the day was the perfect example of the difficulties shooting on the West Coast. Upon arrival, the crew found they had a fully overcast afternoon, a fog layer in fact. Within two hours, the sun came out. 'It created a continuity nightmare,' says Wally Pfister. 'The end result in the film, with the very first exterior segment, there's a direct cut from complete cloud to sunlight. It's a cringe moment for me, but most people wouldn't notice. In fact, it went away on video because we were able to play with the contrast.'

Nolan remembers that day as 'a nightmare' too; aware that the perfectionist Pfister is still bothered by the discrepancy, he knows, as a director, that he had to keep his DP filming:

> At the end of the day, I think it cuts fine; I think it still bothers him,
> but as a director you have to remain aware of the way people
> watch films. They don't tend to look at those types of things. I
> would have to confess, on that day, a couple of shots I would've
> liked to have used, I couldn't, because we had to shoot so late in
> the day, the lighting had changed. Some of the stuff just wouldn't
> cut. Wally, as a good DP, is very aware of what you can get away
> with and what you can't. Sometimes I have to make him shoot
> things that we really didn't know if they'd work.

Day 16: The ShotMaker day. Eleven car sequences were completed over this time; with Callum Keith Rennie back on set, the shot of the Jag and the LandCruiser pulling over was completed; Teddy and Leonard's discussion about cars, in the grey sedan and Leonard in the pick-up truck (in black-and-white) were also completed. Several interior Jag colour shots were done, including Leonard discovering where Dodd was staying from the note, as well as telling Teddy they are heading to the derelict house. Teddy's obtrusive knock on the windscreen was also captured.

For the driving sequences, Pfister preferred to shoot at the right time of day, having carefully chosen the street locations, rather than light heavily outside. By this point, entering into early fall, the sun stays fairly low, but Pfister still shot many of these sequences in the late afternoon. Towing the Jaguar car with the ShotMaker, the crew were able to shoot through the windscreen and side windows with the intention of keeping a natural look. When parked, as with the scene between Teddy and Leonard, after the latter has left Natalie's house, Pfister deliberately kept the lighting 'soft and ambient', eschewing any sunlight patches entering the car.

Day 17: Dodd's motel scenes were shot here. The sequence where Leonard discovers a bound-and-gagged Dodd, and Teddy arrives, was followed by the fight sequence, and then Leonard's wait in the bathroom.

Day 18: A move to the tattoo parlour was next, calling for the arrival of Marianne Muellerleile on set. All her scenes were shot in one day: Leonard showing her the file card; Teddy's arrival; the completion of the licence-plate tattoo; Teddy warning Leonard to get out of town; and Leonard, alone, checking his Polaroids to see that his 'friend' is lying.

Day 19: A very complex day. Firstly, the crew returned to the set of Leonard's apartment, to film the death of the wife. Curiously, on the shooting schedule, alongside the call for Pearce, Fox, plus a masked stuntman, is a call for Pantoliano, who does not make an appearance in the scene. Quite what Nolan wanted to imply with a shot of Teddy in the scene is obscure, but its use would've undoubtedly left further questions hanging over the film's back-story.

'We never filmed anything of Teddy in the bathroom,' confirms Nolan. 'With the direct flashbacks, I tried to vary them to show the way his present state is affecting his memory. This was done by juxtaposing the images in odd ways – such as cutting to his wife as he's about to kill Jimmy. At some point, it was certainly something I had considered, some kind of device where Leonard would visualize a person.'

Pfister calls the bathroom a 'brighter, see-more environment' in comparison to other sets. That said, there is something rather dirty about the light that falls on the Shelbys' bathroom. Pfister was particularly taken with white tiles on the floor. He sees it as the result of him, editor Dody Dorn, production designer Patti Podesta and Nolan himself working 'in synch' on the film. 'The white tiles on the floor are something you see early on – the camera moving across them – and then when it comes back again, after the wife is seen to be killed, those octagonal tiles are like a memory trigger. They're also like little brain cells, in my mind.'

The film then moved to the interior of the derelict building, where Teddy's reverse-murder was to be shot. Nolan admits he was having a hard time conveying how he wanted the sequence to play out, as it could not be shot in one and simply reversed:

> That sequence, it was essential to me that it was conceived as a series of shots, as they appear on screen. Not just shoot a sequence where a guy gets shot in the head, and then wind it backwards. It would be a very different sequence. If you literally just reverse it and watch it backwards, it doesn't work with the timing and rhythm. I knew it wouldn't work. You'd just have an optical effect. You wouldn't have a series of forwards-running shots that combine to give you this backwards effect. For example, the sounds are all forwards sounds. When the shell-casing starts to move on the ground, it's a forward sound. We can't hear backwards sounds. I wanted people to watch it as a physical sequence. If you reverse the sound, the physicality is gone. I wanted a realistic physical scene that happens to be chronologically reversed.

The most tricky moment was with the shell-casing, which drops on the floor – though in reverse flies back up in the air. Neither Nolan nor his crew, could get the metal casing to stop in frame:

> I got on my hands and knees and blew it out the frame, to have the effect of the backwards shot. In the confusion of it all, they shot it backwards as well, so I got it the wrong way round. It gave me a huge headache. I saw it in dailies, and I knew it was wrong but I couldn't remember why, but we figured it out in the editing. So we

had to then make an optical, and reverse the shot, so that it was forwards. That was the height of complexity in terms of the film: an optical to make a backwards running shot forwards, and the forwards shot is a simulation of a backwards shot.

Day 20: Staying on the set of the derelict building, Larry Holden returned to complete his scenes as Jimmy. The fight was shot first, and Holden recalls just how he and Pearce decided to recreate a *Fight Club* sense of authenticity.

'Right before we shot the footage of him strangling me, Guy said: "Hey, Larry. Do you wanna . . . ya know, go for it, so to speak?" In my mind, I was like, "Finally, an actor who isn't a big pussy, worrying about getting some little bruise or cut on his pretty little mug." So I smiled and said, "Sure. Bring it on, pal," and he did. Oh boy, did he. Nearly killed me for real, the bastard. For a guy his size, he's one strong fucking dingo.'

Scenes then shot were: Leonard taking Jimmy's clothes; Leonard dragging Jimmy's body down to the basement; Leonard watching Teddy arrive; Leonard leading Teddy to the basement, and Leonard getting the jump on Teddy.

Day 21: Once again, at the derelict building in the interior, the complex expositional scene was finally filmed, where Teddy tells Leonard that he killed his own wife.

The derelict hallway itself was one of Pfister's favourite sets designed by Patti Podesta, though the one he spent the longest thinking about in terms of lighting it. 'We were restrained by budget, in terms of being able to have anything outside of the doors. Patti came up with the concept of breaking the set in two, so we'd have the derelict hall, and then a separate set for going downstairs into the basement; and also came up with the idea of hanging this plastic over the doors. I had to overexpose the doors on both ends, so that we didn't see outside to the stage, where there was no dressing. It worked for Chris.' Pfister needed to keep the walls dark, to contrast the dingy interior with the bright doorways. It meant – when the camera was in the hallway looking towards the light source – that detail on the actor's face would be lost, as it was held in silhouette. 'We needed to create more detail. So I requested Patti cut a series of holes in the wall that became part of the design of the hallway, where I could put light through, and have little slivers of light coming through the sides of the walls, as if it's an exterior space. That allowed me to put these little pools of light on Guy, but while maintaining this really dark contrast in there.'

Day 22: Again on set at the house, Leonard's fight with Teddy was filmed.

By now, Chris was well aware of the difference between making *Memento* and the one-day-a-week he spent on *Following*. 'This was much more intense. Fast and furious. You had to think much quicker. The pressure of time per day was the same, but the accumulative pressure was worse. On *Following*, I was able to take a week, get a tape on the Tuesday, and edit it together in my mind during the week.'

Day 23: Back to motel room 304, and a number of colour scenes were completed: Leonard preparing to leave to hunt down Teddy was followed by the moment when Leonard believes he has found his killer. The scenes where Leonard calls the escort service, the blonde arrives, he instructs her and then – at night – collects the props were also shot. This was then topped off with the moment when Leonard finds the blonde sniffing coke in the bathroom.

Days 24 and 25: All in black-and-white, the final two days of the shoot were in motel room 21, where Leonard talks on the phone to Teddy and Burt, and shaves and tattoos his leg. Significantly, Guy Pearce had been on set now for every shooting day.

'The state of mind that Leonard is in is, in some ways, like a falsehood he creates in himself, where there's almost a terribly relaxed quality that he carries with him in order to get through the day and every waking moment,' says Pearce. 'One of the things I found when I fell into the making of *Memento* was that because of having to act like this, I felt more relaxed working [every day], when I am there as much as the crew, rather than having days off.'

Following the film's official wrap, Leonard's early narration was shot. Unlike the voice-over for the colour sequences, or even Leonard's over-the-phone narration, this v.o. in the black-and-white sequences was loosely scripted, allowing Pearce the freedom to riff on the lines (a good example being Leonard's wry little comment that he reads the Gideon Bible religiously; in the script, just the Bible is mentioned).

'I wanted to have voice-over reflecting the documentary style,' says Nolan. 'So the way to get that, even though they were scripted was to then improvise on the basis of that script, with Guy, and have him speak about himself in the second person: you do this, you do that, as if he were describing his life to an interviewer.' Edited in the manner of documentary voice-overs, which tend to use a dense information stream, the end result achieved a level of spontaneity Nolan was looking for. 'On some level, it lets the audience know they are receiving objective information; you're finding out more about how this guy lives. Then you jump back into the colour sequences – which are much more obscure.'

Chapter 5

'Just get these clothes on.'
Dressing *Memento*

The production design

Greg Araki's 1999 romantic comedy *Splendor* marked a move away from the bleak Generation-X films, like *The Living End* and *The Doom Generation*, which he had made his name with. Set around a contemporary love-triangle, it was also production designer Patti Podesta's second collaboration with Araki, after completing work on his full-throttle punk-spirited 1997 effort *Nowhere*. Minus the garish pinks and oranges of that film, *Splendor* was a more restrained affair, but after Chris Nolan saw the film at the Sundance festival the year *Following* was at Slamdance, he immediately became interested in securing Podesta's services for *Memento*.

'It was a very different style to what I was looking for for this film, but it was incredibly stylish-looking, and I knew was made for a very reasonable budget. I was really looking for someone with a tremendous imagination, particularly in terms of use of colour – a designer who could achieve a great style without spending a huge amount of money.'

As it turns out, both were at several of the same parties during the festival, though never met. Podesta was actually contacted through her agent, and asked if she wanted to come and meet Nolan, who – having never worked with a designer on *Following* – was entering into uncharted territory himself. Podesta, with no idea what *Memento* was about, received the script. 'My agent was out of town, and her assistant sent it over,' she recalls. 'When I got it, I rang back and said, "How did I get lucky enough to get sent this?" I thought it was brilliant; one of the best scripts I'd ever read. I remember thinking the structure – what people are now calling a "gimmick" – was really baffling. Was he gonna keep this up, or he is gonna play with it?'

Podesta herself was surprised that she got the call from Nolan in the first place, with little in her portfolio to convince him she could design a film like *Memento*. Born and raised in LA, Podesta had originally envisioned becoming an architect, before taking up sculpture and then embarking on a lengthy career as a video artist. 'I got more and more interested in narrative. I then directed something with real good actors in, but I didn't enjoy working with actors – I cared more about the background, and I realized I made films about the things you're supposed to make films with. I was making films about scenery.' Realizing her talents lay in designing scenery, rather than shooting it, she switched to production design, initially working on commercials, before moving into features with low-budget taxi-driver story *Driven*.

With her only other film credits being the Araki movies, Podesta was impressed that Nolan could see past the fact she hadn't tackled a project like this before. 'Although none of my work looked like what he had in mind, he knew that he and I understood each other, and he felt that I would be able to give him the look he wanted.' Not, it would seem, her usual experience in the industry. 'Y'know, if you haven't designed hamburgers, but you've designed hotdogs, they won't let you design their hamburgers. But Chris isn't like that. He thought *Splendor* was a beautifully designed film, with an idea being followed through all the way through it.' Many of the portfolios he had looked at had, as Podesta terms it, a 'kind of realism equalling grittiness'. Her work, as she points out, is commonly described as having 'clarity', a feature Nolan wanted for *Memento* and one that echoed the work of Wally Pfister.

'In regards to clarity and my work, I tend to have things always fairly uncluttered, and try to really have the frame be composed,' says Podesta. 'This comes about from a lot of research, and not by putting a lot of ageing on things. If things are aged, they aren't grimy, they aren't dark. A lot of low-budget designers, who are up-and-coming, do this. You can see it in the action thriller movie, where everybody thinks it should look like *Blade Runner*. And the way they interpret *Blade Runner* is to make everything really muddy.'

A part-time teacher of art and design, Podesta demonstrated a deep conceptual understanding of *Memento*, more so than anyone else Nolan had interviewed. She showed him some still photography, that she describes as 'photo-realism', and also the black-and-white paintings of German artist Gerhard Richter. Talking to the illuminating Podesta, it becomes clear just how much her contribution enhanced Nolan's film. Weaving a motif of wavy glass and transparent plastic through the film, the ideas behind the question of memory are reflected through her design. Think of the shower curtain that acts as a makeshift casket for Leonard's wife; the frosted-glass partition in Dodd's bathroom; the plastic that hangs at the back of the derelict hallway; Natalie's distinct glass tumbler, or the layer of dirt that obscures vision through the Jaguar windscreen:

> Things are diffused and defocused but not by virtue of defocusing the camera. With all of these things, memory makes the image be diffused without the lighting or the camera; it's actual materials that we used for the set dressing to bring that quality to the frame. Those were the ideas that I presented to him when I first met him. I really understood, without even knowing him, the issues in the script. This was all without being explicit, without these things being symbols. That's not something I'm interested in at all, and neither is Chris.

Nolan wanted to 're-define realism' with the film's production design. 'You never know what someone means [when they say that] until they start making choices,' says Podesta. 'Then you weigh and measure the choices.' The pair talked about the look of certain Seventies British movies, including John Schlesinger's 1971 psychological drama *Sunday, Bloody Sunday*. The story of a *ménage à trois* between a Jewish doctor, a career woman and a twenty-something artist, its dour, drab, almost colourless production design (by Luciana Arrighi) achieved the clarity that Nolan was seeking.

'I was very emphatic that *Memento* would need realistic textures,' he says:

> In a sense, I was interested in expanding on something I started to do in *Following*, which was to take theatrical, melodramatic material – the tropes of *film noir*: the guy in the motel room with the gun in a drawer, the *femme fatale* – and try to imply a more mundane, textured and real visual approach. There is stylization – light, shadow and all the rest, but at the same time, there is an everyday quality to it. That was really important to me. It's all very grounded in that contemporary world, and I think very often that when this kind of material is approached these days it's treated in pure nostalgic terms. I was interested in doing something more contemporary, rooted in the everyday.

Chris, it must be noted, is not interested in *vérité* realism per se, the kind we might associate with the work of Ken Loach, for example. But he wanted to use elements of it: 'I just want to take certain aspects, and use it to achieve more everyday qualities of the setting, and trying to contrast that with the theatricality.' The effect is to ground Leonard's experience in the commonplace, an environment stripped of anything remarkable, enabling the audience to empathize with this morally dubious character. At the same time, when required, Nolan – as Podesta points out – would move the film away from this.

'I realized that through the period we worked together – and I think this is clear in the film – that sometimes the need for emotional story-telling takes precedence over the true quality of *vérité* realism for Chris. The emotional quality is implicit as opposed to the story, which is explicit; it's like a piece of music, coming from the design. You have to feel like you're in the world, and yet it is actually quite altered.'

Podesta, while trying not to think too hard about other films, also found herself drawn to the work of Nicolas Roeg. While Roeg is the director considered by many to be Nolan's predecessor, Podesta never discussed him with her director. 'I didn't realize until later that every-body thinks about Nicolas Roeg when they think about Chris! I was thinking particularly about, once again, this question of clarity in *Don't Look Now*. The quality of the red and how soft it is, but how crisp at the same time. It feels like a memory, or a certain kind of image, or a colour, or a sound. That's one of the things I was trying to get.'

Aside from composer David Julyan, Podesta was one of the first key crew members to start working, with seven weeks of pre-production to complete the bulk of the set decoration. One of the earliest – and lengthiest – discussions was on the colour palette that the film would follow:

> Chris wanted all blue, and, actually, I said 'No!' I said 'You don't really want to do that. You want there to be some shadings, that are off-blue. You don't have to bring in other strong colours, but you want different blues.' There are scenes where the blues are quite bright, and there are other scenes where it becomes more green. The blues in the motel room are quite primary, actually; they are quite a true blue. At Natalie's house, the colours are more muted; they're more towards dusky green – and that slows it down a little bit. It was all slight shadings. We took a lot of care in shooting the colours in the black-and-white scenes; we used the same colours so they would have an 'equal' quality – so that time is, in a certain sense, standing still, and the rest of the world is

moving forward. We're caught in this encapsulated thing where most of the world seems to be of the same nature – even though it's not.

It's a colour motif that Nolan sticks with; the bath salts that spill on the floor during the attack on Leonard and his wife; the panelling on the dilapidated building across the street from Natalie's house; the blue-green bottles at Ferdy's Bar; Leonard's bedspread and so on. 'Y'know, once you start, it's kinda hard to stop,' shrugs Nolan. 'It was just something I thought would work with the material. I was quite drawn to the idea of using slightly colder colours, particularly given that we had to film in LA, which is very hot and sunny. A lot of our exteriors are very hot and dusty, and we are trying to counter that in some way, by using the cooler tones, like blue.'

Given also that Nolan is red/green colour-blind, it was also a colour he was very responsive too. With *Memento* being shot on a new Kodak print stock particularly responsive to blue, the resulting palette becomes very distinct, an echo of how Nolan himself sees the world.

What is startling about Podesta's production design is the fact that much of it is achieved on a set. Built on a sound stage at Glendale, in the east of Los Angeles, three motel rooms were constructed (the two Burt rents to Leonard, and Dodd's) to dimensions that resembled the real thing. 'There was a lot of work on the part of Wally and Chris to make them smaller than would be comfortable,' says Podesta. 'It made the space both claustrophobic and realistic.' Nolan and Pfister would also shoot all 360 degrees of the sets, which meant all angles of the rooms had to be dressed and ready to go at a moment's notice. 'It all had to work, because there were no dead areas. Usually on set, there are dead areas. That was another quality that makes you think it's not a set, because you can look at it in any direction.'

Podesta adds that the rooms contained a number of recognizable features, such as the tumblers topped with paper lids, but the design was such that their placement was near subliminal. 'As opposed to other film-makers – who would dwell on those things – in this case, you see them as the camera pans round, but you don't actually look at them. The things are there, but they don't become symbols for something.' To achieve the look she wanted, Podesta had a friend visit a number of seedy hotel rooms in Southern California, and take photographs of the disarray they were left in when the occupants were out. 'We were looking for the state of undress that people leave their rooms in,' says Podesta. 'The state of the walls in unfreshly painted hotel rooms. Those kinds of qualities are very specific and you can't make it up in some way. A lot of times, those things were too down for Chris's idea of realism.'

Podesta's other main contribution was working on the derelict hallway, where Leonard would slaughter both Teddy and Jimmy. It was, in fact, two sets: a hallway with a room and a doorway that led to the basement. The basement itself was up on a platform, which – for purely practical reasons – enforced Podesta's visual motif of diffusion to come into play. Draping plastic in the doorway to disguise the fact there was a roof on the other side, it lent the set a 'limbo' feeling, as Podesta puts it:

> We did a lot of texturing. We applied twenty coats of this transparent colour, to get these clear but deep layers of colour. There were a lot of different textures, but they were all pulled together with this monochromatic colour. So you have visual texture, but you don't have the capacity to see things clearly. You don't see the tiles; you see colour and a bit of texture. It's a corridor with plastic at either end! You could take that as some kind of philosophical thing. It's a very mundane transition.

Her time on the film also included one week to design the tattoos that would be seen on Leonard. 'There are very few styles that people actually use for tattooing. And we looked at them; we looked at pictures of tribal tattoos. The one on his solar plexus, that is a triangle, is actually mimicked after a Borneo tattoo – a ritualistic prayer of sorts.' One stunt Nolan would not be pulling, however, was to change the tattoos around on Leonard's body to disorientate the audience (as Martin Scorsese reputedly did with Robert De Niro in *Cape Fear*). 'Chris did not want to do those kinds of things. In regards to the question of memory, I suggested things like one time seeing the cup as blue, and the next time, the cup is red. He specifically did not want to do any of that. The question of perception and memory was in the structure of the film.'

While only briefly glimpsed in the film, some of Leonard's tattoos are clues to how he has managed to survive with his condition. Alongside the mirror-reversed 'John G raped and murdered your wife' and the inciting 'Find him and kill him' are more everyday instructions. On his belly, upside down, is the command 'Eat'. Advice as to how to train his mind comes with 'Condition yourself', while practical notes like 'Buy film' are adjacent to more philosophical statements like 'Cameras don't lie', 'Memory is treachery', 'I'm no different' and 'Consider the source'. Most fascinating is the aforementioned triangle – actually a series of boxes, each containing a word: 'Photograph', 'House', 'Car', 'Friend', 'Foe'. Guy Pearce, who was required to come to the set three hours early to have the tattoos applied and touched up, remembers the strain he went through in wearing them:

> They took a long time to put on. They printed them first on paper, reserved them and sprayed them on your skin and touched them up if necessary and powdered them down and they would last for five days if you didn't scrub yourself too hard in the shower. So we were constantly having to fix the odd one or two, so they took a long time. It became a great team effort but it happens all the time on films that you've got people fussing round you. I'm a really grumpy person sometimes. If I'm not in the mood for it I have to tune out. These people are doing their job and doing what they have to do.

An essential ingredient to the film's success would be the Polaroids, and it was left to the props department to organize these. A duplicator was obtained, which meant a single photograph could be taken and numerous copies made for multiple takes. 'The duplicates were not great,' says Wally Pfister, who had met Podesta years back on a short called *Spud*. 'The colour was pretty horrendous on them; quite often it was really magenta and muddy. I was not happy with the look of these in pre-production. I went to Chris and Patti and I said I didn't know how well they would photograph. So we just had to live with it. Then we decided that we kinda liked the way it looked. They had their own creepy look to them – a lack of detail with a weird colour situation. In the end, they worked pretty well.'

Pfister ran tests on the Polaroids, partly to determine how to shoot the film's opening scene when the picture of Teddy undevelops. Initially unsure how long they wanted the sequence on screen, Pfister shot at six frames per second, then at 12 and then at 24 (with a reverse magazine). Ultimately, with the scene cut to the titles, the 24fps shot was used, though it was discovered that by manipulating the temperature that the Polaroid was at, its development speed could be altered.

Working without an art director, Podesta was still completing her tasks when the shoot began. Neither Dodd's room nor the Shelbys' bathroom had been locked by the time filming was under way, and Podesta had to work on both while the crew shot elsewhere. The aforementioned bathroom, with its octagonal tiles that Wally Pfister was so fond of, is the perfect example of Podesta's design ethos on *Memento*: the lone black tile that the camera glides over is real, not, as she puts it, 'a movie' tile. 'We knew that we would be looking real close on it constantly, so I insisted that it be a real tile. You can look at it. I knew that we would be looking at things in really precise focus. You had to be able to look at the surfaces, and not be out of the picture, where you would think, "Oh, it's a movie table, or a movie wall." So you're not distracted by it.'

For Nolan, the appearance of the tile was crucial. While we initially only see one black octagonal tile, in the early rapid cuts to Leonard's wife's attack, in the extended sequence where Leonard is beaten over the head and falls to the floor facing his wife, the camera glides on to a patch of floor where two black tiles are visible. Without ever announcing themselves as symbols, the presence of both – aside from figuratively representing the two heads on the floor – seems to tug at us, pulling us towards the idea that maybe double meaning exists throughout this story.

'It's a fairly standard tile that I've always liked,' Nolan says. 'It's very textured and the tiles are very small, and each individual black tile is spaced quite widely, so when you shoot it from above you just get one or two popping into frame, which seemed a really interesting image that would stick in the head and later be explained. You feel you know where that image has come from. It's another way of putting abstract images through the film that later become clearer.'

Overall, Podesta was surprised at 'the level of shared comprehension' she had with 'a first-timer' like Nolan. 'It was largely unspoken and completely understood,' she says. 'I was able to talk candidly with him about what I wanted; usually there's a power thing that goes on, as people stake their territory. Designers are the first people to block things, when you lay out a room, working out where the furniture goes. You automatically design what the shots will look like, in a certain way. Here, there was not a lot of territory, but there was a lot of sharing.'

The costumes
Memento must be one of the few films where the lead character has no clothes of his own. Like Arnold Schwarzenegger's killing machine,

in *Terminator 2: Judgment Day*, Leonard (a terminator in his own right, also out of time) takes the garments of another. Only with the unreliable flashback to his work as an insurance investigator do we see anything that could be taken as Leonard's own attire. In the colour sequences, he is wearing Jimmy's beige suit and blue shirt, while the black-and-white motel scenes see him dressed in a plaid work shirt (liberated from his previous victim, one may assume). Even accidentally dressing in Natalie's ill-fitting white shirt at one point, Leonard's cerebral confusion is echoed in his state of (un)dress. Though the style remains contemporary, there is something distinctly timeless about the clothing; togs that don't easily slip out of fashion – nor are they often in vogue – they hint at the warped time-loop Leonard finds himself in.

Nolan was adamant that Leonard's main set of borrowed clothes remain 'a beige suit and a blue shirt', as the script states. 'It was an outfit I used to wear all the time,' he admits:

> Not as a suit, but I had a beige jacket and a blue shirt. As I was writing, for the same reasons I would wear it, I put it in the script. It's kind of in the middle; it's not like wearing a suit with a tie, or a black jacket with a white shirt. It's right in the middle and a little bit difficult to get a handle on the character when you see him dressed that way in the film. It's ambiguous. It could be smart, or could be more casual. That was what I was after, something neutral. It could be worn, as it is at the end, by a drug dealer in a slightly flashy way, with the collar splayed outside it. Or as it looks on him, larger and more stylish, in a baggy way. It doesn't give you a clue as to who the guy is.

If nothing else, it gives us a clue to Nolan's own personality: his dress sense, like his work, remains ambiguous, giving little away. *Memento*'s costume designer Cindy Evans, as one would expect, sensed the relationship between Leonard and Chris's apparel. 'Chris dresses a lot like that. He always would wear a suit jacket, even if it was 120 degrees. It was really nice. And I only ever met one other director like that, and that was Andrew Niccol on *Gattaca*.'

Evans had been brought on to the project by Jennifer Todd. The pair had a mutual friend, who persuaded Todd to let Evans read the script and meet Chris. 'Cindy was a costume designer I'd known for a long time who I wanted to give a break to,' confirms Todd. 'She was someone

I believed in. I hadn't worked with her, but I had known of her for a while. She had worked on a bunch of movies for Jersey Films, for my friend Stacey Sher. She was somebody I'd always wanted to break in.'

Texas-born, Evans grew up in Lake Sherwood, where she would regularly get to see *Dukes of Hazard* being shot. 'I got the bug at a really early age,' she says. 'We'd sneak behind oak trees and watch what they were doing. I was always intrigued.' With no training to speak of ('I'm self-taught, most of us are.'), Evans – after a stint working for John Candy when he made *Planes, Trains and Automobiles* – began working under three times Oscar-nominated costumer designer Colleen Atwood. This included time on Tom Hanks's nostalgic directorial debut *That Thing You Do!* and, as mentioned, Niccol's genes-thriller *Gattaca* – a film that Evans admits was in her mind when on *Memento*. 'I don't think I styled it after *Gattaca*, but it had an oddness and a coldness that *Gattaca* had. There was something about *Gattaca* that I realized too when I was making *Memento*. I always felt *Memento*, even though it was really low-budget, was something special.'

With just one feature credit as costume designer to her name (Eric Drilling's low-budget film *Red River* – 'my budget was about $3000!', she recalls), Evans was aware that *Memento* was her big break. Like all the key crew members, she read the script a handful of times:

Boy, was it intimidating. My brain felt like it was going to bleed. When you get a project, you immediately start wanting to break it down in chronological order to find out how many costume changes there are, and how many different days there are, and what days lead into night. Even the first time you read a script, you're trying to constantly absorb that. And so, on the first time I read it, I was like, 'Oh, my God! What is this?!' I became obsessed by it, and I finally began to understand the fragmented structure, and the continuity came later. I remember I had become so familiar with the material, and even if I didn't understand the structure, I began to understand the characters, and where they came from and what they were doing. I honestly, first and second time, was completely lost. And I'm not embarrassed to say that.

Evans impressed Nolan in their initial meeting with the sheer wealth of research she had undertaken beforehand. She had watched *Following* on tape: 'I really loved it, but I wish I could've had my hands on the wardrobe, though. Just the girl. I loved the guys' stuff.' She also spent time thinking about the look of *film noir*. 'I think Chris and I had a few of the same sensibilities, with what the characters were going to look like in the film. We tried to accommodate that desire to make it a more modern *noir*, and I think we achieved it. Chris really wanted that feeling of a timeless look. I really wanted the same thing, but [I was] trying to achieve that in a really subtle way. I think *Pulp Fiction* achieved that, in a modern sense.' Most intriguing for Nolan was *Mr. Salesman*, a coffee-table book published by Diane Keaton, that Evans brought to their first meeting. Full of photos from the 1950s of various besuited businessman, it particularly captured the look that Evans believed best represented Leonard as an insurance investigator. 'We took a lot of the black-and-white stuff from Guy Pearce's point of view, when they are testing Sammy Jankis, from the textures of that book: the striped shirts, and the starkness from it. His look was very kempt, very insurance salesman. A little on the tidier side than what you normally see. Boring, really.'

With just over a month of pre-production time, Evans – along with two assistants, Laura Marolakos and Anne Laoparadonchai – set about assembling the wardrobe for the cast. With a relatively small number of main characters, few extras and a contemporary setting to boot, one could imagine *Memento* lacking the logistical complexity of a film like, say, *Titanic*, making it a relatively simple job for a costume designer. Evans would be the first to agree. But, in terms of calculating the number of costume changes the characters would need, the project was far from a pushover. With no obvious references to day/night in the script, Nolan's backwards structure obscures the number of days that the action takes place over – thus making it nightmarish for the costume designer to decide how many changes a character might need. Evans recalls the early days in their production office:

We shared a mutual office space with the art department, and the props department. The ADs were on one side, and Wally [Pfister, DP] was on the other side. We could all hear each other, all day long, trying to work things out, all theorizing. It was amazing. It really helped so much. I can't imagine being in an office on your own trying to work that out. When Chris came down he would give everyone the time they needed. He loved answering the questions, and he loved to hear the confusion. He would get this twinkle in his eye, this Machiavellian look, this funny grin, as if this was exactly what he planned!

As it happened, Emma Thomas had provided a continuity breakdown for the key crew members. Generally a job the first AD and/or script supervisor would be given, to provide people with a time-line to work from, it was decided that Emma, being so familiar with the script and having it on her computer, would re-order it chronologically. Says Emma: 'It took a couple of days during which I felt as though my brain had been replaced with a ball of string, but I got there in the end! Chris was hugely opposed to the idea of people having copies of the "chronological" script, but it seemed that we had to do something to get everyone on the same page; so I kept the *one* copy of the re-ordered script under lock and key, but used it to create a chronological time-line by scene number which we then distributed to all the departments.'

For those interested, the action – barring flashbacks – takes place over three days and two nights. The time-line itself is still under lock and key along with the one copy of the re-ordered script, and neither Chris nor Emma is currently accepting bribes. As for Cindy, the time-line was a godsend. Despite Leonard largely remaining in the one suit, seven outfits were made, covering three different states of wear-and-tear. Naturally, with the film going backwards, Evans had to contend with the fact that the suit gets cleaner as the movie progresses. Not a problem in itself, except for the fact that – as with most productions – *Memento* was shot out of sequence.

> Guy changed so many times through the day, because they might do twelve scenes a day, back and forth across the whole film, so we were constantly triple-checking that he was in the right suit. Maybe the audience doesn't catch that the suit is getting cleaner and cleaner, but that is what we were trying to achieve. I kinda think we did. I took all the black-and-white stuff out of the script, and cut it out, and then I re-copied it and then I broke everything down into segments. I had a wall-chart at one point. It was quite a challenge I have to say. I started living and breathing it. I felt so good about it, when I finally felt like I had broken through that first door.

By comparison, actually ageing the suits was as easy as wearing them. Which, oddly enough, is what Evans spent most of her pre-production time doing:

> I remember Chris and Emma came over one afternoon, to see how the ageing process was coming along, and I was wearing the pants!

I was constantly rubbing the pockets, with this oil that I had on my fingers. That's my favourite part. It's really, really time-consuming, but it's the only way you can do it, and make it look really good, if you have a lot of time. You just can't throw a load of dirt at it. Everything was about textures. The suiting fabric we tested, but I used the reverse side because it had a file detail to it. It appears more raised that way.

As Evans notes, Leonard has a very dusty look about him; unspecific, his suit may be Armani, but you're never quite sure, leaving you uncertain about Leonard's own background. 'If you look at the pockets on the suit, they are flat pockets; the suit is not really tailored to be severe with shoulder pads, or anything,' she says. 'It's a very loose-fitting suit. The guy obviously had a little bit of money, but I don't think he was desperately loaded.' It's testament to Evans's work that we do not initially realize Leonard is wearing another's clothing, though upon closer inspection it becomes obvious. 'With Guy, he was always more dishevelled. The size was always a little bit odd to the eye. As you get closer to the end of the film, you realize his whole look never looked right on him. I think when we came to film the suit on Jimmy, I thought it definitely looked a lot sharper and cleaner, and more put together.'

Larry Holden, who plays Jimmy, disagreed, uncertain about his tan-coloured apparel and jewellery. 'I look like shit in light colours. I'm too fucking white. And I wasn't big on the chain around his neck, either. Felt like it was a little much – but I was alone there, because everybody that's seen the film has commented favourably on both the suit and the chain and my fucking moustache. So, it shows you what I know.'

With Leonard's blue shirt, however, in keeping with Patti Podesta's indigo-tinted production design, Evans thought she might encounter difficulties. 'I was really scared of the colour blue. I had worked with so many costume designers, and blue is their least favourite colour. It's really difficult to time it out, once the film is colour-graded. It ends up looking purple. There are so many degrees of blue. In the dailies, I was like, "Aggh!" and Chris said, "What's the matter?" And I said, "It's so blue!" It really worked out beautifully in the end.'

For Nolan, costuming was considered more on a thematic level. Dealing with issues of identity, clothing becomes an astute way of symbolizing how we identify ourselves. 'One of the interesting questions for me is, "What are your own clothes?"' says Nolan. 'There are a lot of things in the film that imply the relationship of the clothes and the car to the action. When we see him with the truck, wearing the plaid shirt, the question hangs over that outfit and car – the same question Teddy asks him in the car: "Where'd you get that?" There are no answers, of course.'

With his decisive use of colour in the film, keeping the palette centred upon shades of blue, Nolan was also able to suggest a great deal during the flashbacks to Leonard's wife, who wears a red summer dress – ultimately as haunting in Leonard's mind as the red-coated figure that spooks Donald Sutherland's character in Nic Roeg's *Don't Look Now*. 'There's very little red in the film at all, until the flashbacks of the wife, with her blood,' says Nolan. 'That's the only time we really highlight that colour. I wanted that to be very specific and evocative about the colours, so we used white and red, in a way that we don't use them in the present tense. All the sheets are greyish; we don't use any pure whites in the film, except in the flashback.'

Pre-production also incorporated the design of both Natalie and Teddy's outfits. For Teddy, Evans was unsure initially if they should give away that he was a plain-clothes cop. Dressed in a bland navy windbreaker, a pair of black Oxfords and cuffed trousers, Teddy's clothing manages to imply his profession, without ever being explicit. 'We wanted to have that look. You look at his car and his clothes, and you know he doesn't have a lot of money. That jacket – it was like a mailman's jacket – reminded me what an "everyday" man would wear.'

Using two sets of doubles for his outfit (his death scene, at the film's outset, required it), Evans recalls that Joe Pantoliano was full of suggestions about clothing his character:

> In his own personal way, he's a huge fashion guy, and he wears clothes really well. It's really hard to say, 'We're going to go shop at Sears or Wal-Mart for you.' These are Everyman clothes; we're not going to go off to Maxfields and buy Teddy's clothes, because it would never make sense. It was about tweaking him in the right direction, and making sure that what he really wanted he got, so he was happy. It is what it is. We didn't have a lot of money. We had to make what was going to work for the movie our first priority. We got him a pair of shoes that he wanted, which were these black

Oxfords, and after that he was like, 'Whatever you want, put them on me!' He was putty in our hands.'

For Pantoliano, dressing Teddy was a part of building the character. An actor who loves to change his looks ('it ensures my longevity as an actor'), he admits to working outside-in, rather than inside-out:

I figured as I was a police officer I needed comfortable shoes; that I would wear a loose shirt, so I could hide my revolver underneath it. I wanted to wear clothing where it would not stand out. I could just blend into a crowd. Chris was also very involved in those choices; usually, you'll work it out with the costume designer and take a Polaroid. But Chris was there. When we chose the glasses, Cindy and the props guy had all these glasses. I knew in my head that I wanted to have bifocals and I wanted that to be clear on the close-ups. I also wanted to have one pair of shoes. That was the start of it. It was important to Chris I had a moustache, and with that, the crew-cut wig and the glasses, it was kind of like a click. OK, listen, there he is.

With Natalie, Evans hit on the idea of dressing her in cold and steely charcoals and gun-metal greys, rather than black, suggesting the ambiguities of her character, rather than painting her as evil personified. She also set about making a lot of her tops transparent, again producing doubles of everything – particularly for the scene where she is hit by Leonard:

You could always see a little bit through her sweaters. You don't really get to see many wide shots of her, so that when it was all cut together, it was really claustrophobic. You didn't get to see a lot of what was below the waist with the characters. Her skirt, I had made from this 1930s kimono, so it was like a wrap-skirt. It was really sheer, and the sweater was really sheer – there was a big hole in it. Everything of hers happened really easily. I had this one photograph I found in this magazine of a woman who had her head tilted down, with this big, black shock of hair. She had her hand through her hair; it was a stance of frustration. From that one photo, I caught into who this character was. It was just like an attitude.

Natalie was also fitted out with a selection of jewellery that Chris wanted to keep small and subtle. Even the earrings couldn't move. It all helped give the character an 'indescribable strength', as Evans puts it. 'She has this strange quality; the sheerness and the clothes made her transparent, but there was something about the jewellery that grounded her for me. It wasn't like the jewellery was wearing her. It was part of her. She had that watch, with that wide leather band, which was like an armour. You never really get to see it for a long time; she's constantly moving, so you'd just get to see flashes.'

Evans spent little time with Carrie-Anne Moss, who was happy to go with the costume designer's ideas. When the fittings came, with Chris in attendance at every stage, the trio were able to watch Natalie come alive. Says Evans: 'There's so much going on with the character's development right there, as a person is putting on the clothes, that you necessarily can't just show a director the photograph, and say that this is what's happening with an outfit. It saved a lot of time, because he's right there. She put on her main outfit, and I said, "This is a home run!" I just knew when she put it on, and she loved it.'

While the bulk of Evans's work was done in pre-production, she still found herself working on costumes for the Jankis couple while the film was shooting. 'As it was in black-and-white, it was all about texture and fabric to keep them Middle American,' she says. 'There were a lot of sweaters, and sweater-vests. It wasn't ever black, but there was a lot of heathered greys, and a lot of plaids going on. She had a lot of floral prints.' Suggesting, once again, bland suburban fashions, Sammy's white shirt and Mrs Jankis's dresses could have been made at any time in the last thirty or forty years, an echo of Leonard's own clothing – and, indeed, another link between Sammy and himself. 'It wasn't hard for me to envision what was going to be happening with these people and these clothes, because their clothes were so subtle,' says Evans. Subtle, yes, but meaningful also.

Locations and lists

By the time Wally Pfister came on board, there was just two weeks of pre-production left. 'That was tight,' he recalls. 'A little too short.' The reason behind this was a major location switch, from Canada to California. At one point, Montreal was to be the city where *Memento* would be shot. When California was settled upon, the increased costs of using an LA crew meant the production schedule was cut from 30 to 25 days.

'I fought very hard for the movie to be shot in LA, and I'm glad that we did,' says Jennifer Todd:

Chris was quite pleased with how the look of the film turned out. I'm always scared of Canada, because people are quite quick to send you there, because of the tax breaks on offer. Suzanne and I are from LA, and I knew that on the outskirts of the city, where we shot, there would be that great look for it. The bummer was it was 100 degrees every day on the set, but I loved that destitute, no-man's land Americana we found. It's very homogenized. You can't tell where you are. It just looks dry and dusty. It could be Arizona, it could be Nevada. Creatively, I always fight on films to be set where the most appropriate place is. [Ben Younger's] *Boiler Room* [which we also produced], for instance, takes place in Manhattan. New Line said it would be cheaper if we shot in LA. I've known movies shot in LA for New York, because there are only two blocks in LA that look anything like Manhattan, and they're used in everything. You end up shooting in these tunnels to try to make it look like Manhattan tunnels. When we did get *Boiler Room* shot in New York, I made sure we had shots of these big water towers so you knew it was on the East Coast. The same way, for this film, we could've shot it in Pheonix, or wherever, but I fought very hard for it not to be Montreal. From what I've seen of Montreal, I didn't think it lent itself to *Memento*. It's always that thing if an extra talks with an accent, it pulls you out of the moment. Stuff like foliage and quality of light . . . there's a lot about the environment that you must take into consideration.

With the majority of his work to come during the shoot, of course, Pfister had just a fortnight to assemble his camera crew, and plot with Nolan how to photograph the movie. 'Really what pre-production is about for me is to get as much of an idea from the director as I can as to how he wants the picture to look. Then to translate that, so we have a verbal shorthand on set. It's not about discussing for hours and hours the look of the picture, while we're sitting on the set. It all should've been done beforehand, in an ideal world.'

One task the pair had to reach a compromise on was the shot-list, usually compiled in pre-production to break down each scene into the coverage needed. 'Shot-lists I never do,' states Nolan. 'Producers make you do them, so we shot-listed the first two days, just to reassure everybody that I knew where I'm going. I don't respond very well to that format. It just doesn't help me. You haven't seen the actors yet in the environment, so it's a reductive thing. The main purpose of it is to communicate with other departments.'

Pfister, who had experience of cranking out shot-lists on previous films, hoped to do one for *Memento*, it being such a complex shoot with only 25 days to capture all the material. While he sensed that Nolan wasn't interested in creating one, he wasn't prepared to push the point, until Jennifer and Suzanne Todd requested one. 'Until this point, I really didn't know whether Chris would know what he was doing on the set either. I knew he had made a film before, but he had made it over a year, shooting on weekends. I was a little bit nervous too and a lot was at stake.' Arriving at Chris's office with his computer, Pfister undertook a page-trim with his director, whereby the pair went through the script, 10 to 15 pages a day. It enabled Pfister to ask all his initial questions, and glean from Nolan just how the film was to be shot. 'As soon as I sat down with Chris, I found he really had a clear idea of how he wanted the film to look. The shot-list, for me, became unnecessary, because I knew that Chris knew what he was doing, and I was comforted.'

Nor was Nolan particularly interested in storyboarding, a process he indulges in only to get him thinking in the right way. 'I get bored with it very quickly,' he says. 'Most [storyboards] are drawn according to conventions, and they have a comic-book feel to them, which doesn't necessarily relate that strongly to where you're going to put the camera, and what lens you're going to use.' For the scenes where Nolan found it difficult articulating what he wanted to other crew members, story-board artist Mark Bristol, who had worked on Nolan's recent favourite *The Thin Red Line*, was used. Most perplexing for Nolan to explain was the opening murder-in-reverse sequence. 'Generally, I'm very good at visualizing things in my head pictorially, shot to shot, but on that scene, I was having a very hard time conveying what I wanted and what would be practical, because there were effects involved. The whole reverse nature of it meant that it was actually very helpful to have the shots as pictures, so I could show people the order in which they were going to take place.'

Pfister also spent some of his pre-production time visiting the locations that had been approved by Nolan. 'We had a wonderful location manager,' he says. 'All those locations were together and locked within that two-week period.' Scouted by Russ Fega, the procedure began weeks before with Podesta, who was shown a selection of locations, before deciding what was or was not appropriate. Initially, Fega wanted the motel to be from the Safari Hotel chain. 'We said, "No, no, no!",' says Podesta. 'We wanted something anonymous. We were looking for locations that were exchangeable with each other, which was not that easy. Chris specifically didn't want it to look like Southern California. He was thinking more of Middle or Northern California. We were looking for a place you could not place. A no-place. A place that is pervasive, everywhere, but you never look at it, for the most part.'

Looking for buildings that were all built in the same period – chiefly, the early 1970s – the motel chosen was actually called The Hillcrest Inn. Based in the middle-class suburban area of Tujunga, north of Los Angeles, it was re-painted with certain signs removed to 'complete the monochromatic quality to it', as Podesta puts it. Nolan, who points out the actual search for the right motel was one of the lengthiest location scouts, specifically wanted a 'motel that pretends to be a chain, that has ripped-off a chain, but is actually family-owned'. While the motel had to be re-named the Discount Inn (one of a number of names Nolan had thought up to imply the inherent shabby nature of the place), Nolan was particularly pleased with the motel they settled for:

> It was such a very, very peculiar design. A courtyard motel, totally enclosed, with these weird bars on some of the entrances. All of the angles of the courtyard are slightly off, so one end is shorter than the other, one balcony is slightly higher than the other. We were limited as to how much we could show of that, but – to me – it's very nice when he leaves his room for the first time, and he goes down the staircase into the office. To me, you really do get this sense of spiralling, cycles, circularity. It's the perfect motel for what we were looking for. You wake up, you walk out the door, and you can't see anything outside of the courtyard. It's totally closed in. Very surreal.

It wasn't entirely set up for shooting, though. While it already had a prison-like quality, even up to the bars on some entrances and paint-stripes above doorways, the feeling of claustrophobia was further created by Podesta, as she continued the paint-stripes across the roof – thus locking Leonard in with a series of verticals and horizontals.

Jonah Nolan was particularly taken with the real residents:

> I remember going up to the motel where Leonard was supposed to be staying, and the characters who were actually staying in the

motel would've made fantastic extras in the film. The people who owned the motel had just rented it out. They took the money and ran. I don't think they even made the customers aware of the fact that the production company would be descending on the motel, closing off the entire premises, forcing people to stay in their rooms, and – of course – turning the air-conditioning off. In September, in the Valley, the wind can blow back in, and it gets red-hot out there. Asking people who live in a residential hotel to do that didn't go over very well. That really felt like you were actually there. Sitting there on the set, you could forget about the camera crew. It felt completely genuine.

For Sammy's house, a suburban house was chosen close to Pasadena and re-dressed. Podesta was automatically drawn to the house because of its large, glass-panelled front door, which helpfully aided her design motif of light diffusion. 'It was quite a ritzy house and very, very big,' she says. 'We had this eight-foot couch to bring the scale back down. There was a half-wall, when you walk in, that divides the room, and made it feel a little bit more compressed. In reality, it was huge, but on camera – behind Sammy – it looked like a little half-wall. Things were over-scaled to make the room feel smaller; that was kind of strange – to show that Sammy was in the space, and surrounded.'

Natalie's house, meanwhile, was in Burbank, in a white picket-fence middle-class neighbourhood, close to *Memento*'s sound stage. 'The thing about Natalie was that she still lived in the house that her parents had occupied, and she was a bit of a pack rat,' says Podesta. 'She really hadn't got rid of their stuff. You can see that in the design and the furniture, which is quite a bit older.' Much work was put into making it look 'a bit down', as Podesta calls it. Re-painted, it was given a new fence and blinds. It entirely fooled Jonah, who arrived in town just as production started.

'Right in the middle of this block was this complete shit-hole. At first it didn't even register, because it looked so natural. You walked inside and there's shit all over the place. It took four or five days, when we had wrapped there, before someone pointed out to me that the fence wasn't real, the colour of the house wasn't real . . . all of it was fake. I was blown away at how people can put these things together in such a way that you wouldn't even notice it.'

The tattoo parlour was not even that; based about three miles away from the motel in Tujunga, the space had just been leased, and was empty. 'When we shot there, all the stuff was still in boxes,' says Podesta. 'It's part of the reasons why the design of the interior has the divider wall, with the tattoo designs on it. In the actual location, you couldn't actually see into the building from the outside; you'd see the reflection of the window. You can't really see into the building 'cos it would be a stage set. That was the way we did that the whole time. Wally did such a great job of melding those moments together.'

As you may have guessed, the name 'Emma's Tattoos' was in honour of Chris's partner, and the film's associate producer, Emma Thomas. 'As with all films, you have to go through the process of clearing every location name, and I can't remember the name of the original parlour – I think it was 'Mary's Tattoos' – but we couldn't clear it. It seemed obvious that there weren't likely to be any other 'Emma's Tattoos' anywhere in the United States, and sure enough there weren't.'

The exterior of the derelict building proved more troublesome. Owned by a train company, it was a Spanish-styled brick building that seemed ideal. A week before shooting began, Podesta sent an assistant down, on a hunch, to see once again what it looked like. Dozens of full-sized train carriages had been placed there by the company since the location had first been scouted, rendering it unusable. 'We had to change locations a week before they were going to shoot the exterior, and we had already built the interior,' says Podesta. 'So we had to find an exterior that would architecturally work with what we had already built, and that I could blend back together.' It also meant scouting a whole new location on a weekend, when filming had begun: 'a nightmare', as Pfister called it.

Russ Fega's alternative suggestion was an oil refinery based in Carson, near Long Beach. 'He was a bit sheepish about suggesting it,' remembers Nolan. 'He said it was way over-used in TV and films. When you go down there and look around the place, it feels too familiar. Way too familiar. It has all these weird different aspects. Right to the left of where we are shooting is this massive, complex oil refinery that you would recognize from every other movie.'

At it happens, with Nolan tracking in and out of the scene as the vehicles approach or leave the area, dwarfed as they are by these three rusty tanks, the location is made to feel quite unique to *Memento*. For the sequence where Leonard burns his wife's things, the same location was used (rather suitably, given what the character is doing in the scene), but on the other side of the over-filmed refinery. 'We were shooting these weird concrete blocks,' says Nolan. 'They looked almost like a graveyard, which was very apt.'

Fortunately, the Ferdy's Bar location proved a lot easier to secure. Called The Blue Room, and located in Burbank just three blocks from the production office, as the name suggests, its colour palette matched Podesta's to a tee; the blue walls and ceiling needing no alteration by the crew. The cafe where Teddy talks about memory with Leonard was actually The Grinder, also in the vicinity. As for the restaurant scene between Natalie and Leonard, an establishment in Pasadena was used, though Podesta once again went to town on the walls, shading them in sea-green – a similiar colour to motel clerk Burt's work shirt.

A book of pictures was then compiled to show to Nolan, who had specific ideas for each location. 'Russ would go out and photograph the locations in a very particular way. He was able to really interpret what I wanted and really come up with interesting ideas. It was tricky because I wasn't looking for the most baroque or unusual locations, which I think people very often are on low-budget films – they're just looking for anything that looks interesting. I was most concerned to find a banal reality that was just skewed enough to express the story, but was very much in the story.'

Chapter 6

'Do you have a pen?'
The Origin of the Film

Memento Mori

So we end at the beginning; the seed of an idea is always the hardest to trace, artists of any sort often reluctant to pinpoint their source of inspiration. Like many films, *Memento* 'is based upon' a literary source. In this case, *Memento Mori*, the short story written by Chris Nolan's younger brother, Jonah. Curiously, the story had not been penned when Chris first heard his brother's premise, on the now-infamous road trip he and Jonah took from Chicago to Los Angeles, when Chris was relocating to the West Coast. As diverse as they are similar, the film and the story began in earnest on this trip, each brother taking the kernel of this tentative idea and exploring it in his own way.

'The story's a funny one,' says Jonah. 'I've been trying to come up with a good set of origins for some time now. The place where it came from was out of a collection of different influences.' When I first speak to Jonah, rather aptly he's on the road, making another trip across country. When we resume our conversation he's house-sitting for Aaron Ryder in Los Angeles. With an accent as American as Chris's is English (he is five and a half years younger, and so spent his scholastic years in the States), he seems to embody the drifter spirit that you just know exists inside Leonard Shelby. He talks like a writer, carefully delineating his story, so you hang on every word.

Back in 1996, while Chris was in England finishing up *Following*, Jonah was over three thousand miles away at Georgetown College, Washington, DC. He had taken a General Psychology class, which, inevitably, led him to thinking about memory loss. 'In Psych classes, they love to talk about "anterograde amnesia" – chronic short-term memory loss. It's not a particularly common affliction in young people. But it does provide a window to the way the human mind works. I found plenty of material devoted to it in the textbooks, so I had that in my head.'

The following semester, just three days into his course in International Relations, he decided he needed time out; hot-footing it to New

Zealand, where some relatives owned a sizeable dairy farm, Jonah decided to work there and clear his head. There he stumbled on a collection of heritage books and picked up Herman Melville's masterpiece *Moby Dick*. Like we all have with books that have stood the test of time, he had many preconceptions about Ahab's battle with the leviathan. 'I always had this idea in the back of my head that it would probably be my favourite book – I don't know why – but I read the thing and, of course, it's clearly my favourite book. It's a book best read when travelling. You're out there, and you're a little bit unnerved yourself. I spent a month and a half reading it and it put me in a state of mind of revenge. That's the seed, and the seed came with me.'

He quit the farm soon after, and, after a spot of hitch-hiking and a Stateside detour, he wound up back in the UK. Deciding to travel Europe, he flew to Madrid with his girlfriend. Arriving late that night, he consulted the guide book for directions to a hostel, which sent them in the wrong direction. Walking in circles through the city, they got picked up by three thugs, looking for easy targets. 'Such as stupid Americans with backpacks!' he guffaws. Aware they were being followed, they pressed on regardless, even stumbling upon a sign for the hostel.

'I think we're home free,' he recalls. 'We cross the street, and wind up in a dark little alley. We arrive at the lobby and there's nothing there. Just a mailbox, and two flights of stairs. Suddenly these three guys are in the lobby, and my girlfriend does the right thing, and tries to bolt out the door. They grabbed her first. They all had knives. Before I know it, my knife is out of my pocket, and I'm being held at the throat with another one.'

As it turns out, the hostel was one flight up, but with the ground floor nothing more than a hollowed-out shell, the crooks could afford to take their time and search through their captives' possessions. 'For the first thirty seconds, I was shit-scared. After thirty seconds, I realized I was six inches taller than all three of these guys. Here they had me in a situation which I knew would bother me for months. It would fuck up the way I travel and I would obsess about it. So I start to get pissed off. And I'm just standing there, with these guys. They're even more scared than I am.'

The trio found a camera and petty change, and scarpered, leaving both parties unharmed but shaken. Spending the evening diffusing, Jonah and his companion did not, as the police suggested, 'do the responsible thing' and visit the station to pick out mugshots. 'I knew I wouldn't be able to pick them out of a crowd,' he says. 'Your eyes are filmed over with anger after thirty seconds, so you're not taking anything in.' Returning to the UK, before later completing the European trip, Jonah felt himself victimized, and the mugging stayed with him. 'It stuck in my head that real life has no resemblance to the movies you grow up watching. In that situation, my kung-fu moves didn't manifest themselves. I didn't have a surge of bravery, which you always figured you would have. It was so quick and so clinical, and then you spend the next three months obsessing over what you could have done.'

Things began to congeal in Jonah's mind as he returned, like the prodigal son as he says, to his parents' London home. 'One night, I was whiling away the rest of my days before I was due to drive back across country with Chris – as he was moving to the States. I was lying on the floor – where my makeshift bed was – and something popped into my mind: this image of a guy in the motel room. He has no idea where he is, and no idea what he's doing, and he looks in the mirror and notices he's covered in tattoos. I couldn't tell you where that came from. But that was what I got.'

Taken as a still – think of the oft-printed publicity shot of Leonard, with Natalie behind him, uncovering his torso to see his own tattoos – it is a shocking and surreal image to arrive in your mind, unaccounted for. It speaks volumes for the ten-minute cycle that Leonard finds himself in, the waking dream he constantly experiences, the repetitive shock of discovering your loved one is dead. It's also an image born for the cinema.

'From the very beginning, I had the idea that this would make a better piece of cinema than it would a piece of writing – even before I had talked to Chris,' says Jonah. 'The first thing that came to mind was not a set of words, but the image. The story wasn't a throw-away. I'm quite happy with what I came up with. But I knew it would come through a bigger form. The idea was truly intended, somewhere down the road, for the cinema.'

Chris himself was particularly taken with the idea of the tattoos. 'When my brother told me the story, I really responded to that. It speaks to me as the most extreme form of recording experience or information.' The picture of a man staring in a mirror also opens up the central question of *Memento*: who we are, and how we perceive ourselves. Undoubtedly, we all have a self-image that differs vastly from how others see us. The raw truth of a mirror is sometimes too much to bear. 'I think most people think about themselves from looking at themselves in pictures, and in the mirror in the morning, and catch glimpses of themselves in the street,' says Jonah. 'When we get closer to what we look like, or what we're doing, it becomes shockingly apparent.'

Prior to driving with Chris across country, Jonah had taken a short camping trip in Maine, which drew his attention to this. When he returned from his sojourn in the woods, he was stunned at what he saw. 'I didn't look at myself in the mirror for eight days. I looked like a wild animal. If you ever see a wild animal up close and personal, they have this sheen of filth all over them. It's not like a domestic animal, it's wild. When I looked in the mirror, that's what I saw: someone I didn't recognize; hair standing up, blemishes, bits of dirt, soap and mud smeared all over me. It was kind of shocking. I don't know what people did before mirrors!'

July came, and it was time to drive. As befits an idea based on memory, the brothers remember it slightly differently. Travelling in their father's old Honda Prelude, Chris recalls Wisconsin, Jonah the 'fairly dreary state' of Minnesota, when the idea was hatched. Either way, the 'homogenous American roadside', as Chris calls it, was there for both to see. Jonah's Chris Isaak tape was stuck in the machine, a perpetual looping sound that appropriately symbolized Leonard's quintessential dilemma. Preparing to tell Chris he was working on something big, Jonah recalls just how nervous he was.

> I'd talked to my brother about ideas before – and met with little success. Chris is the kind of guy who doesn't get enthusiastic about things. He doesn't bullshit you around much. The idea had been rolling around for a while, and I was quite happy with it. Sure enough, I got lucky and he thought it was pretty cool. We kept driving, and we kept talking. The funny things was, he immediately started to turn it around in his head. My brother is one of these people . . . he would probably attribute it to his left-handed ability. He has an odd first way of looking at things. The second you pitch him an idea, he'll start reversing things and inverting them. I don't really know where that comes from, but it's a certain skill he has. He puts it together as an object he can handle; he rotates it, flips it around. It's in his head so clear he can see it in three dimensions.

Got a name for it? Chris asks. *Memento Mori* – it means 'remember to die', says Jonah. Won't work for a film, Chris thinks. 'Great title,' he says. Within minutes, Chris was thinking of the film in terms of a screenplay. He didn't know whether Jonah would permit him to have a crack. 'You never know when somebody has an idea that personal and that good whether they want to sit on it and figure it out for themselves, as he clearly hadn't. He knew the story. He didn't know the form, or quite what he was going to do with it. In retrospect, he may have told it to me because of that. He was looking for somebody to take it in a different direction, and do their own thing.'

In retrospect, Chris was not surprised to hear that Jonah was nervous about confiding in his older sibling. Ideas are fragile things, he says. 'Anytime you tell anybody an idea that you think is important or interesting, you're actually putting a lot on the line. If somebody shoots one down, it's gone for ever.' A series of concepts not yet fully formed, Nolan knows just how difficult it is to articulate to another at this crucial stage. 'It's a bit like trying to remember a dream, and trying to explain it. It makes it so much less than what it was in your mind.' Sensitive to his brother's needs, Nolan was also aware of a time when the situations were reversed:

I showed him the screenplay for *Following*, and we talked about it. Whenever I've shown him things, he's always had interesting advice and it tends to stick in my head. The thing I always remember is that he said, 'The only way it will work is if it's incredibly fast and efficient.' Which the screenplay was anyway. He had tapped into what I was trying to do, which was tell the story with no padding, just the bare bones. That banged around in my head for a long time. It was very useful advice, and confirmed what I thought of the material, but when you get that external confirmation, it bolsters you.

The remainder of the summer, the brothers were apart, Chris in LA, Jonah back in DC, preparing for college. Chris, already wrestling with the idea, wanted to see Jonah's first draft. 'He kept hassling me,' says Jonah:

I sent him a very rough first draft at the end of the summer. It was just bits and pieces, the nuts and bolts of the story. It was about five pages of notes and descriptions and narrative – which was actually what the final story would look like. I was trying to tackle the same problems he was; which person, which tone, which tense, do you employ to try and tell the story of a man with no short-term memory? How do you make that happen? We both thought using first person was the way; the most interesting way of doing it. Really getting inside his head. Not looking at him from an outside perspective, like telling the story through the eyes of a police investigator, or whatever. I was stumbling with that, in terms of writing, trying to figure out a way to do it. I came up in the end with a dialogue that was between first and third person.

Chris's urgency came from wanting to start writing, and not feeling he would be able to until he had read Jonah's first draft to use as 'a jumping-off point', rather than basing it simply on their conversations. 'I eventually convinced him to send me a draft, which was an early draft,' says Chris. 'I was immediately struck by several of the images he had put in; things I had already decided that would go in the screenplay.'

Call it shared consciousness or sibling symbiosis, but both Jonah and Chris hit on similar ideas at points without having discussed them with each other. In the first draft of the story, a line about a shower curtain is used as a metaphor for the description of the killing. 'I'm actually quite squeamish about thinking of those kinds of things,' explains Jonah. 'But Chris had already come up, independently, of this idea that the wife would get caught behind a shower curtain.'

According to Jonah, Chris wasn't particularly enamoured by the name Earl for the protagonist. 'My brother called me up one day and said he thought the name Earl was stupid! Naming characters is hard; coming up with something that doesn't sound too artificial, but is interesting and memorable. I got stuck using Earl over and over again; I don't quite know where I got it from. Chris had a different take on it, and he came up with Leonard.'

Memento Mori is most certainly recognizable as the blueprint for *Memento*, but not merely because it concerns a man with short-term memory loss who lost his wife in a brutal murder. Evocative and poignant, it juggles with the same themes and ideas as the screenplay, but emerges with a distinct slant on them. In terms of tone, Jonah's writing contains the same grim humour that is found in his brother's screenplay. 'Must be a hell of a story, if only you could remember any of it,' we hear, recalling the numerous 'memory' gags made at Leonard's expense. Earl, it seems, has a healthy manner of provoking himself; practical notes are pinned around his room, for when he's just blazed up a cigarette, that read: 'Check for lit ones first, stupid!' Later on, the humour blackens, as Earl is told, with his condition, he can no longer have a normal life, and hold down a job: 'Not too many professions value forgetfulness. Prostitution, maybe. Politics, of course.' Equally, his images are chosen with a degree of perspicacity, describing Earl/Leonard in a way that his brother's screenplay can only hint at, such as the state of purgatory he has reached. Explaining what Earl has left, we are told he lives with his 'finite collection of memories, carefully polishing each one', his past life 'set behind glass and pinned to cardboard like a collection of exotic insects'. Also delighting in ambiguity wherever possible, Jonah uses 'maybe' whenever he can. 'Maybe then he notices the scar'; 'Maybe you can't understand what happened to you'; even the weather is either early spring or late autumn, 'one or the other'.

Set, partly, in the hospital that Earl is admitted to after losing his wife, it can be viewed as back-story to Leonard in some way, an account of how he first geared himself up to setting out on a quest for revenge. As we are told in the final words of the story, 'If this moment is repeated enough, if you keep trying – and you have to keep trying – eventually you will come across the next item on your list.' In other words, with no short-term memory to speak of, motivating yourself to such a deadly assignment is a laborious and methodical task. Emphasizing the cyclical nature of Earl's predicament, twice we see him staring at the photo of himself at his wife's funeral, to show the perpetual nature of his quest. Jonah draws comparisons between Earl and Man, each of us being 'broken into twenty-four hour fractions'. Earl/Leonard's 'fraction' is a great deal smaller, of course, but the principal of writing a list of instructions to combat this problem is the same. While Earl needs to work his way through a series of commands just to function, we all need a list to combat the variety of personalities that tussle with each other inside of us. 'Every man is a mob, a chain gang of idiots,' we are told; the sex-addict, followed by the introvert, and the conversationalist, and so on. Only briefly, every day, do we reach a moment of clarity, or 'genius', where the 'secrets of the universe' are open to us. To remain in tune with this state, we need 'a master plan'; steps to repeat ad infinitum to keep us aligned with the planets, as it were.

In many ways, it intensifies the Earl/Leonard character's daily problems, detailing the highly structured routine he must go through each day. Alternating, as Jonah said, between first and third person, the story, chronologically speaking, switches between past and present.

The first-person segments are written by Earl to himself; an account of how an 'earlier version' tries desperately to pen explanatory notes that will be found later on by himself, in the hope that – with his recent memory fading away – they will incite him into action. In the bathroom, for example, he finds one that says: 'If you can still read this, then you're a fucking coward.' On the back, it says 'PS. After you've read this, hide it again.' Written with the knowledge that ,within minutes or hours, Earl will not remember what he has just done, the tone of the voice is weary, hinting at how futile the exercise really is. As he says: 'It's a shame, really, that you and I will never meet. But, like the song says, "By the time you read this note, I'll be gone."'

At one point, the 'former' version of Earl buys a bell to carry around, in the hope that it will remind him – through conditioning – of his predicament (not unlike the 'Remember Sammy Jankis' tattoo). As an example, we read an anecdote about ancient burial-sites, where the rich – fearful of being buried alive – would have a piece of string running from coffin through an air-tube to ground level. On the surface, the string would be attached to a bell which could be rung if, by some chance, the deceased turned out to be alive. Earl's bell, of course, is purchased to help remind him he is alive, retrieve him from the dead, as it were.

Opening with an apt quote from Melville – 'What like a bullet can undeceive!' – that recalls Leonard's slaughter of Teddy at the film's outset, there are a number of parallel moments in story and screenplay. Scenes that can be recognized, in some way, in the final film include Earl noticing an arrow on his wrist, which leads him to unbutton his shirt and unveil the tattoos to remind him of his quest (including a police sketch of the assailant on his chest); the desperate search for a pen, as he tries to record information permanently (in this case, having just killed the man he believes to have murdered his wife); Earl's system of Post-it notes, resembling Leonard's maps and Polaroids; and his visits to the tattoo parlour.

The story also introduces the motive of revenge – and how it relates to time. While *Memento* has Leonard deliver the 'How can I heal?' speech, highlighting how he has no concept of time and thus is repeatedly struck by grief, *Memento Mori* informs us that Earl is unable to forgive, because he 'can't remember to forget', a line Leonard also utters when burning his wife's things. Time, we are told, for most people is 'three things' (past, present and future). For Earl, it is just the present, the moment he lives in. Calling him the 'ten-minute man', the story preempts Chris Nolan's structural device, whereby scenes do not last longer than this amount of time, to keep us within Leonard's 'present' moment. Symbolized by the absence of a watch on his wrist – after all, that was for 'the you that believed in time' – Earl is a man out of time.

Chris, rightly, believes that the screenplay and the short story arrive at the same place, but in both different ways and different manners:

> We arrived at two methods of storytelling – one in the short-story, and one in the film – that, when you analyse them, are clearly related, in terms of the alternations between subjective and objective, but they're arrived at in completely different ways. I didn't set out, for example, to write a story that alternated subjective and objective. I set out to write a story that looped backwards. That was my job. Jonah's was, even in the early draft, an alternation between first and third person; the dialogue between two souls.

For Jonah the following year of college was a blur, punctuated by his external correspondence with Chris, who was toiling away on the screenplay. Jonah continued writing and revising his story; a number of versions exist, one passed out to people before production on *Memento* began, and a later effort, penned while Chris was editing. It was this that would later be published by *Esquire* magazine – a deal that had been struck after Emma Thomas had contacted a number of publishers on Jonah's behalf. 'She is much more sensible than I am and more acutely aware that I will need to put a career together,' he says. 'I remember I was in an airport lounge in Bangkok, after a few weeks in Thailand. Got an e-mail from her saying *Esquire* had bit, so I did my little dance around Bangkok International airport.'

Jonah's revisions were a process of experimentation, his pages a writer's playground. He recalls the introduction to an anthology of amnesia fiction he later came across. 'The [intro] talks about first-time writers being drawn to amnesia because of their own psychological condition, staring at a blank piece of paper. Most typical amnesia stories begin with a character staring at four blank walls.' Jonah, as is clear, already had his idea solidly ingrained in his head. Despite settling upon the more-than-adequate dialogue he used between third and first person, Jonah carried on playing, hoping to send tremors through the lit-crit world, aware that – just like an idea – once published, a story is in the public realm and cannot be recalled. 'My original intention with the book – trying to re-invent the entire form, which most writers try and do early in their career – was to decide that page-reading wasn't good enough,' he laughs. As mentioned in connection to his conception for the website, he briefly pursued a deck-of-cards format, offering the reader the chance to shuffle the pages and investigate the story from a series of randomly ordered perspectives. 'No one does this with books, but they do with magazines, flicking through to find the article they want,' says Jonah. 'Chris, as he's left-handed, has this thing where he reads magazines backwards.'

The screenplay
It's an interesting – though admittedly moot – point as to whether *Memento* would ever have been written had Nolan stayed in London, rather than moving to Los Angeles. Undoubtedly, Jonah would have shared the idea at some point, but there would have been no cross-country road trip as an excuse to tell it. More importantly, unlike *Following* – which is a very London-centric movie – a UK-set *Memento* would not have worked.

'It wouldn't have been the same film,' contests Emma Thomas. 'He didn't write it until he moved to LA, and a lot of the themes of the film, in terms of anonymity, I don't think would've translated to England. I don't think you could set it in quite the same way over there. Here, in California, you can drive all the way up to San Francisco, and not really know that you're in a different part of the state. There are lots of small towns that have the same basic buildings, like Dennys and Motel 6. You just don't get that in England in quite the same way.'

Chris sees the story as a quintessentially American one, dependent on being set in a vast country with an identifiable homogenous culture. 'There's something about the landscape. It's not specifically LA. We shot around Southern California. There's really nothing in the film that you could recognize as LA. That seemed very important to the story, to be getting lost in this landscape. There is a sense that the setting, and the relationship between the setting and the predicament of the character is very American.'

His new-found home proving the perfect artistic inspiration, Nolan set his mind to the problem of telling a story about a man with short-term memory loss. No more than two months after he had received Jonah's first draft, he excitedly called his brother long-distance with the notion of how to tell Leonard's tale: sdrawkcab.

'He told me that and there was a long pause,' says Jonah:

He probably waited for me to say something, and I think I wound up saying something polite, rather than informative. I did think for a little while that he was off his rocker. I thought he was nuts! I thought he was being silly. I thought it was an extension of his impulse to invert things. At the time, I wasn't familiar with Pinter's *Betrayal*, the *Seinfeld* episode, Martin Amis's *Time's Arrow*. It did strike me as a pretty novel concept, but also as such a simple idea that surely it must've been tried before and surely it must've failed.

As already noted, Chris had read the Amis novel, but had seen neither Pinter's play nor, indeed, the episode of US comedy *Seinfeld* that ran backwards, and claims not to have even been aware of them at the time. 'If I ever had, I never would've done it, because you would have said, "Well, someone's done that,"' he reasons. 'That's part of the creative process for me. I don't watch other films, or read too many other books. You just try and go deep into your own mind. It feels very much at times like somebody else has done everything that you might come up with. I don't waste any time worrying about that. In trying to decide how to visualize it, I had plenty of influences I wasn't aware of while I was doing that. In retrospect, once you've finished the film, you go back and look at it, and you can see other films feeding into the material.'

Unquestionably, Nolan is working very much from the tradition – 'the structural adventurousness' – instigated by the likes of Sidney Lumet and Nicolas Roeg in the 1970s. Films like Lumet's *The Offence* and Roeg's *Bad Timing* and *Don't Look Now*, Nolan had seen when he was younger, and were undoubtedly buried in his subconscious when he was thinking about *Memento*. Roeg's 1980 film *Bad Timing* – the grim tale of a torrid affair conducted between a psychoanalyst (Art Garfunkel) and a woman (Theresa Russell) he meets in Vienna – has more in common with Nolan's *Following*, with its triple time-line. With the film roughly divided into three stages, each section flashes forward or back in time, crossing the time-span of the relationship, which culminates in an act of necrophilia. Less structured than *Following*, the disorientating narrative has the effect of dislocating the characters from the world around them. In many ways, such an effect is also achieved with *Memento* – the backwards-structure reducing Leonard's experience to the 'present', setting him adrift in time.

Lumet's 1972 film, the story of a policeman (Sean Connery) who cracks under the weight of the gruesome sights he must contend with on a daily basis, makes an interesting comparison to *Memento*. Hinging on the interrogation of Baxter (Ian Bannen), a suspected paedophile, by Connery's acerbic, embittered Detective Sergeant Johnson, John Hopkins' screenplay sets out to reconstruct through memory what went between them both. As Trevor Howard's probing superior states, 'I have to find something like the truth,' the key word being 'like', suggesting – like *Memento* – that 'truth' is a subjective concept. By the conclusion, it is suggested Johnson has tendencies like Baxter's, as he asks him if the paedophile's mind is full of 'thoughts, shadows and darkness' (as, we infer, is Johnson's). Bannen's paedophile – the Sammy to Johnson's Leonard, perhaps – even has two scratches on his face, like Leonard.

Whether Nolan meant such tributes or not during the writing process, on the surface his thought processes worked on a more immediate level. 'What I do is sit there and think, "What do I want to do? What story do I want to tell? And how do I want to tell it?" The reason I was so excited to arrive at the idea of telling the story backwards was simply that I'd been struggling to find some kind of solution to the problem I'd set myself of telling the story of someone who can't remember in the first person.'

He recalls the moment when the idea first came to him. The Honda Prelude that they had driven across country in had just broken down the night before. Sitting at home, that day, waiting for Aaron Ryder and Emma to return home and take him to the mechanic to discuss the plight of their vehicle ('It was dead!' he sombrely recalls), he began to get the feeling of an idea. 'You just sit with it for a little while. You know that feeling when you really crack something? That it's gonna go somewhere. Emma and Aaron came home at lunch to pick me up and I told them both, 'I've just had the kind of idea I only get about every two years or so,' which is true – that seems to be my pace of creativity. I didn't tell them what it was.' Ideas, after all, are fragile.

After the triple time-line structure for *Following*, to go backwards would seem the next logical step for Nolan, whose theory of film narrative revolves around re-training the audience to view the flow of information presented in a different way. After fifty years of being fed linear stories on television, Nolan believes the medium has held back the development of the visual narrative:

Things are simpler now than they were back then. I really think it's TV. It's entirely linear, it has to be. It's changing now, but you have to be able to watch the last ten minutes where they explain

169

the whole story, so you are narratively satisfied. As soon as VHS came along, you could control the time-line – when you watch it. The actual experience of film might well have pushed much further if not for having to be compatible with people's expectations of this visual medium. People get used to watching TV in that way.

Highly influenced by Graham Swift's novel *Waterland*, Nolan points out that the non-chronological structure that Swift employs would never be questioned by novel readers, for it's simply accepted as common literary practice. Prior to the widespread introduction of television, Nolan believes film had the potential to go the same way. 'Think of *Citizen Kane* now. The narrative structure is incredibly inventive. Every other aspect of film-making, since that film, has advanced enormously. I now have incredible editing freedom that people making films back then didn't have. I can have an incredibly fractured *mise-en-scène* that people can put together like that. But narratively, things are simpler now than they ever were.'

In many ways, Nolan's belief in the freedom that prose literature can achieve has been wound tightly into *Memento*'s narrative. He calls a book 'a possessory experience', meaning that it can be re-read until the reader is satisfied with his or her understanding of the writer's intentions. He cites Jonah's story, as an example. 'It's a very bare bones story. It's the kind of thing that works very well as a story, as it hints at this much bigger thing you could grow it into. Kind of the point of this story was to suggest things to you and allow you to mull it over. People are much happier doing that with a short story or a novel than they are with films.' As it turns out, *Memento* emerges as a film that people have been more than happy to revisit and mull over.

Keeping regular writing hours – 'I don't write in the middle of the night. I don't do anything in the middle of the night. I never got into those crazy hours' – Nolan wrote the screenplay on a computer (unlike *Following*), which enabled him to easily check how it would read chronologically. He did not begin constructing the screenplay, though, until he had thought out his ideas thoroughly:

I won't write something until it's ready. There are people who religiously write a few pages every day; I'll get to that in a project. Once you've got 30 or 40 pages in, you have to start disciplining yourself, otherwise you'll never finish. Scripts are very hard to write, in terms of that it is very hard to sustain your interest, once you've done the exciting bits. That's another reason why on some projects you don't fully form where the story is going to go, because you don't quite know yet. I think *Memento* was right in between; I knew more or less where it was going because of the cyclical nature of the story, so I felt free to dive into it, but I didn't really know where it was going plot-wise.

What was clear, by this point, though, was how a man with short-term memory loss could function in the real world, or at least in the world of a cinematic narrative. 'I knew he would need an extraordinary focus of energy and a specific goal for his life that could never be let go of. For Leonard, in a way, the worst thing that could happen to him is to achieve his quest, because then he's left with nothing. For me, that's quite a compelling way to look at the way somebody lives their life; the things that they use as points of focus to distract themselves from the bigger picture, as it were, their place in the universe, if you like.'

To anchor Leonard's story, Nolan used the crucial Sammy Jankis sub-plot, ostensibly a means of showing the audience a character with the same condition in a more everyday setting, how it would appear in the banal reality of life when not on, as Chris puts it, a 'crazy quest'. For Nolan, it was vital the script acknowledge the extraordinary nature of the Leonard situation, its melodramatic nature. 'If we acknowledge that in the film, which I think we do through the Sammy story, we're suggesting to people that a lot of the melodrama is subjective. If you step outside the condition, and you view it in a different character in a totally different context, it takes on a very, very different feel, and you feel very differently to the Sammy Jankis character than you do towards Leonard. To me that was an important contrast.' Until Teddy suggests 'Sammy didn't have a wife,' Leonard's former client becomes a touchstone for what not to do. It is a way for Leonard to understand his own condition, and master it, by recalling Sammy's failure to cope with the disease. 'Sammy had no drive. No reason to make it work,' says Leonard. When Teddy drops his bomb-shell, it sends Leonard into free-fall as his fragile sense of self is attacked by external 'facts' that impinge upon his own dismembering of the truth.

While both siblings did some research on the condition of 'anterograde amnesia' to grasp the basics, Chris deliberately avoided examining the case studies they found too specifically:

As a writer, I don't want to be Tom Clancy. I'd rather just make it up, otherwise it was in danger of becoming a medical thriller. The condition is a real condition but I don't present it in a realistic fashion. The film is an exaggeration of this condition for its metaphorical potential. I didn't want to feel too hemmed in, in terms of where I could take the story with this protagonist. I thought such a condition would provide a character and a very interesting point of view from which to tell this story.

Jonah concurs, explaining that Leonard becomes a metaphor for how everybody is and how everybody leads their life. By way of explanation, he recalls one line from the original draft of his story that survived, to some extent, in the final film: 'After all, everybody else needs mirrors to remind themselves who they are.' Chris's screenplay warps it slightly: 'We all need mirrors to remind ourselves who we are. I'm no different,' says Leonard near the end. Jonah remembers this revision took on an alternative, bleaker meaning than was first meant. 'Originally, it was about a guy trying to reassure himself that he's really not that different from other people. In the film, that line has darker significance. No one really has any idea who the hell they are.'

Chris had originally attempted to expand on the idea, with a line that said, 'We all need calendars to tell us what day it is.' Deciding it did not have the same tone as Jonah's line, he returned to the idea of the mirror, and the process of self-identification – something that began when his brother, of course, had spent a week in the wild without seeing his reflection. 'That fundamental idea that every day you use this device to essentially remind yourself what you look like is absurd. In the case of Leonard, he's pointing out at the end that he uses more crutches than the rest of us, but we all use those crutches. I just thought it was such a striking notion, so I decided to save it for the end of the film, and to have it said by him in a context where he isn't in front of a mirror. It becomes much more something he's thought about again and again.'

As demonstrated in his perceptive essay, Dion Tubrett recgonises that the mirror is ultimately John G. 'As the narrative reveals, [he] is a kind of mirror for Leonard: a mirror-image, the inverse of Leonard; and a double, an external embodiment of his negative attributes.'* As he goes on to point out, Leonard's double remains unseen and has no

' Tubrett, Dion, 'So Where Are You?: On Memento, Memory, and the Sincerity of Self-Deception,' Cineaction, Issue 56

independent identity; he simply becomes Lenny's motivation to live.

On a more personal level, Leonard's obsessive zeal to find his wife's killers is a reflection of the film-maker's own drive to carry through a project. 'For me, the process of film-making is all about obsessional behaviour,' says Nolan. 'Directors, I think, after they have made a film, are put in the position of the protagonist of this film, in that they're having to focus on immediate day-to-day issues, but always trying to place those issues in the context of an overall scheme of things that one is trying to visualize in one's head. I think in the process of making any film, directors are required to be intensely focused on a particular mental image they wish to achieve, and that is very similar to Leonard.'

What is initially hard to detect with Nolan's screenplay is the conventional sub-structure that runs underneath the narrative's backwards-motion. Set in three acts, the twist arrives right on time, as we discover Leonard is imprisoned in a perpetual cycle of revenge. 'I did that deliberately, thinking that people weren't going to notice,' says Nolan. 'To me it was important to create a film that people couldn't watch in a passive way. They actually can, but they get a very different film, and they do get an emotional journey, if you like. I've shown it to people who don't care about plot, and they get a lot out of it; they have an emotional experience, and accept the confusion as a clear part of what you're meant to be experiencing, and follow the rhythm of the piece.'

Jonah's early scepticism towards Chris's idea of a backwards film would later disappear as Chris began sending him pages through. 'That first scene, on that first page, I'll never forget reading that. With the Polaroid snapping back in the camera, and the head reassembling itself, it's a real moment. I'd never read or thought about anything quite like it.' Trouble was, with Chris's words impinging on Jonah's mind, it made working on his own version of the story difficult. 'I found myself sitting there consciously trying to erase my memory of what my brother had put together.' While the story kicked off the screenplay, the script got fed back into the story and vice versa, the two informing each other. Jonah gives an example:

> I'm a pretty good bullshit artist, and the way to do this is if you tell
> the most interesting story, compellingly, it becomes gospel. The
> most flamboyant version of events, told well, becomes what
> happened. To a certain extent, this is what Leonard is doing in the

film. And what Earl is doing to himself in the story. He's telling his version much better than these police reports can, in a way that's much more believable.

By the time Jonah read the first draft of Chris's script, in the Spring of 1998, he was hooked. He describes the process of watching his brother work on his own idea as 'like feeding a virus into a Petri dish and watching it multiply'. He cites the Sammy Jankis story, as an example: 'That had nothing to do with what I came up with. I really don't know where he got it from. It's a little frightening. People talk about that as the emotional core of the film, which is understandable, as the whole point of Leonard is that he's manufacturing emotion, to a certain extent. He has emotional responses, but because he can't connect chronologically with what happened, they're sort of arbitrary. He props up his own emotions.'

Astounded that his brother, in the space of seven months, had taken his idea and spun a dense, 170-page screenplay, Jonah still wasn't surprised at the direction Chris was heading in. 'It's interesting to see how two different people – with similar minds – would treat it, one as a story, one as a film. To me, the broader strokes, and more important points are there. You can see Chris's fingerprints; you can see the way in which he was wrapping this story around *film noir*, and his understanding of film.'

Emma Thomas, meanwhile, remembers seeing the same early draft. 'He must have found it a frustrating experience, because I sat there on the couch and read the script, tutting, going, "Oh, my God!" and flicking back through the pages to work out where I was. I don't think he was overly happy about that. From that point, even until the last week of shooting, it was a work in progress. He was working on different areas of the script. He definitely played with it, structurally, to make it easier to understand.'

For Nolan, the rest of his time was spent simplifying the screenplay, particularly in terms of thinning out the plot. Much that was specified in the original draft, wisely, now remains hinted at in the finished film. In the first draft, for example, Leonard stayed in two different motels, to indicate more explicitly the cyclical nature of his story. To prevent unnecessary complications, two motels became two rooms at the same motel. The character of Burt was, in fact, two characters initially. 'In my mind, they'd always been the same character anyway, so it was easy to strip that down,' says Nolan.

While the Sammy Jankis sub-plot that Jonah was so taken with was there from the beginning, it had been truncated from how it was first written. Nolan had started out with a number of scenes relating to the notion of appetite, where Mrs Jankis had stopped feeding Sammy to see if he'd remember to eat. 'People who lose their memories potentially don't, because the weird thing with hunger is that you stop feeling hungry after a point. You don't recognize what you're feeling,' says Nolan. 'I had all those things represented visually: hiding a sandwich away and showing him where it was, and then returning to the house to see if it's still there.' The finished film only contains the briefest of references to the story, as Leonard's voice-over tells us: 'It had got to the point where she'd get Sammy to hide food all around the house, then stop feeding him to see if his hunger would make him remember where he'd hidden the stuff.' Interestingly, some lines cut from Teddy and Leonard's conversation in the diner also revolved around food, again strengthening the link between Jankis and Shelby. 'I never know if I've already eaten, so I always just eat small amounts,' says Leonard, adding, 'It's weird, but if you don't eat for a while then your body stops being hungry. You get sort of shaky but you don't realize you haven't eaten.'

Largely, though, the first draft and the completed movie remain within touching distance of each other; the backwards-structure meaning (as Chris would find out during the editing process) that it became difficult to remove central scenes. Only another two drafts were produced, each fresh one slightly less dense, before Chris was ready to show the script to others. Aaron Ryder, who then lived opposite Chris and Emma, was one of the first.

'I thought "Wow!" This is the most complex script I've ever seen. It was 150 pages. It was incredibly dense, as you can imagine. You couldn't pick up on the structure until about 30 pages in, because the way it was told was so visual. At the same time, I knew it was one of the most innovative scripts I had ever seen. I said that countless times, as I sent it to agents. It was an amazing blueprint for what would become a great film.'

The making of Memento
Ryder had arrived in Los Angeles in 1994, having trained as a director at Emerson College. Employed by Working Title, initially as a production assistant, Ryder worked on Stephen Frears' The Hi-Lo Country, the

Coen brothers' *The Big Lebowski*, as well as the worldwide smash *Bean*. It was here he struck up a telephone relationship with Chris's then-girl-friend Emma Thomas, who worked at the London office. Offered a job in the development department of the LA branch, Emma arrived in the city in the spring of 1997, oddly enough filling the position just vacated by Ryder, who had since been head-hunted by Newmarket. A financing company that had invested on a limited basis in such cutting-edge fare as *Dead Man* and *The Usual Suspects*, Newmarket, as we have said, had just fully financed their first film, *Cruel Intentions*. Ryder was hired to find new projects for the company to fund; little did he suspect that one would be living in the mind of his next-door neighbour.

Ryder, of course, had been introduced to Chris by Emma, when he arrived in July, full of thoughts about *Memento*. 'She brought with her her boyfriend – who had just finished making his movie on weekends, with a shoestring budget,' he recalls. 'Just what Los Angeles needed – yet another resident film-maker!' Ryder's cynicism soon evaporated when he saw what Chris had achieved with *Following*:

When I first saw *Following* I was truly impressed. I knew how he had made it before he showed me the film. I always hate watching films friends of mine have made, because you're always put in that awkward position if it's no good. My wife and I watched it on the Sunday night, and were so impressed. Clearly this guy knew exactly what he was doing. That was enhanced by the fact that he shot the film one day a week. That movie is not a linear film at all. I think the structure is far more complex than in *Memento*.

By the time he read the script for *Memento* – 'perhaps the most innovative script I had ever seen' – he and Nolan were firm friends. Ryder was determined to get the film made, and he took the script – along with another, for 'this small movie called *The Mexican*' – to his bosses, Will Tyrer and Chris Ball.

Everybody here internally at Newmarket saw how great this film could be. No one had ever read a script like it. We were all very, very excited about it. Everybody initially was concerned about its commercial viability, but it was what it was. We weren't trying to go out and make an incredibly commercial movie. This was the same company, after all, that had financed *Dead Man* and *Velvet Goldmine*. We weren't just seeking movies like *Cruel Intentions*.

It's great to have a balance of commercial films and ones you are really proud of. This company has taken a lot of chances on first-time film-makers.

Nolan's script was optioned immediately, and Ryder then set about ensuring that Newmarket would mitigate the financial risk as much as possible. With a $4.5 million budget set, Summit Entertainment were, as we have seen, brought on board to handle the foreign sales. The next step was to bring on board a producer. Ryder suggested Team Todd, the sister team of Jennifer and Suzanne, behind the *Austin Powers* films. 'My feeling was the script could be seen as incredibly esoteric, an art film,' says Ryder. 'It needed a commercial sensibility to it. Team Todd, through their associations with *Austin Powers*, bring that commercial sensibility and credibility, too.'

Despite this, Jennifer Todd maintains that Team Todd is an outfit that is best known for smaller-budget pictures, including HBO-portmanteau drama *If These Walls Could Talk* and its sequel. 'The first *Austin Powers* was a $16.5 million film; it was only the second one that got fat! Suzanne and I tend to work in the smaller realm. We had been with Newmarket for a while, and we got lucky that we were offered *Memento* – and we were smart enough to hang on to it.'

Jennifer remembers reading the script, while in New York, working on Ben Younger's junior Wall Street drama *Boiler Room*. 'I thought it was kinda crazy. I got into bed quite late, with the script, and I started to read it, flipping forwards and backwards. And I thought, "Oh God, I'll never put this down!" So I started again in the morning, 'cos it was way too confusing. I thought it was really cool and ambitious. I wasn't 100 per cent positive that it would be the film it ended up being, but I thought it was worth a try.'

Obtaining a copy of *Following*, Todd – along with her sister, who was partly wrapped up with post-production on *Boiler Room* – began to assess just what sort of film-maker this young British-American unknown was:

[As a producer] your job is to decide whether to take on a project like this. You sit in a room and you meet with somebody, and you have to go with your instincts as to whether they'll steer the movie in a good direction. I really had a lot of confidence in Chris after I met him. When I came back to LA, I sat down with him and my sister, and we thought he was really smart. We knew he had a very clear vision with what he wanted to do with *Memento*. You often find that with writer-directors, because they're not interpreting someone else's dream. It's their own dream, and you just have to feed off that dream. That was very much the case with Chris.

The Todds' main job, once on board, was to help Chris crew the film, as well as assist him in calculating how to shoot the film in 25 days. As a means to put Nolan at ease, Emma Thomas was hired as production associate. With only London-based composer David Julyan brought on from the *Following* team, Thomas – who co-produced that film, with Nolan and lead actor Jeremy Theobald – provided a reassuring link for her boyfriend. Having met each other while in the same halls of residence at University College, London (Thomas was studying History), they both joined the university's esteemed film society. While there, aside from producing the shorts *Larceny* and *Doodlebug*, Nolan and Thomas made the feature-length *Larry Mahoney*, the story of a lonely student who finds an address book and works his way through it, pretending he's someone else. With both also making appearances on screen, the film was a dry run for establishing a working method for *Following* – Nolan's slick directorial debut.

'*Larry Mahoney* was less regimented, because we were still at university, so we were doing it at night-time,' says Thomas. '*Following* was altogether a different animal. By that stage, we were all out of university, and the biggest challenge was keeping it going over such a long period of time. Keeping everyone interested, and keeping our actors' hair the same length! We had to change our methods slightly, from that perspective. Ultimately, because it was the same people working on it – other than the actors – the working method was pretty similar.'

While not with *Memento* from the beginning – 'I was still at Working Title – somebody had to pay the rent!' she notes – Thomas proved a worthy addition to the team. During production her task was to protect Chris. 'I was always there, and if Chris had any problems or worries, he would tell me and I would go and deal with them. I would be the liaison between Newmarket and the Todds. The way Chris works is that he's very, very focused, and he can't think of anything other than what he's shooting that day. I was there to be the conduit between him and them.'

In pre-production, she, along with numerous others, worked on the film's ending. The script itself needed little alteration by this stage. Jennifer

Todd recalls she 'had the least amount of story notes and changes on any movie'. But she was concerned at how open-ended the conclusion was. A fortnight before shooting began, Nolan himself realized this, and came to Jennifer Todd wanting to, as she puts it, make Teddy 'more specific at the end'. She was relieved. 'Giving Teddy the dialogue about what he claims is the truth was great, because it wasn't that specific before.'

Throughout each draft, Nolan had been simplifying the action, and providing more answers to each plot question. Adjusting the film's finale was, in his eyes, simply the conclusion to this process. 'Theoretically, it supplied the audience with more answers – and I think it's very important that we have the answers to those questions. And that's how it's always been constructed. [The screenplay is] not deliberately contradictory. We were very disciplined in the way we constructed the plotting, and the answers to those questions.' That said, Nolan was always keen to cloud over certain parts of Leonard's back-story:

> When Jonah and I first discussed the project, even from our first conversation, it was very clear that the whole point of the story was such that explicit confirmation of what had happened to this guy between receiving a blow to the head and the present day would always be obscure. Otherwise, you'd be cheating the audience. It *has* to be obscure. Or uncertain, at least, even if it's theoretically clarified by a character or a prop, or whatever.

During the two-week rehearsal period – something Guy Pearce calls 'really valuable' on a film fraught with continuity details such as *Memento* – he and Nolan would meet at Joe Pantoliano's house to thrash out the final scene. Allowing Pantoliano to ad-lib, as he would on set, Nolan let his actors feel their way through the scene. 'A lot of my dialogue, Chris was smart and confident enough to let me make more of my own,' says Pantoliano. 'It was quite proper and I wanted to Americanize it. He was very easy about that. We would talk it out, work it out. It was really a great way to work; I would like to work that way in the future.'

With Emma joining them in Pantoliano's Santa Monica office to work through the script in the run-up to the shoot, the ending proved to be a process of refinement and revision even throughout the film's shoot. One other person contributed ideas: Jonah Nolan. Fitting, perhaps, that the man who inspired the project should help conclude it. 'It was really brilliant having Jonah around,' says Thomas. 'He was definitely a collaborator at the script stage. He had lots of brilliant ideas, clarifying or giving the script different layers of meaning.'

Jonah turned up in town the weekend before shooting commenced. With Pearce also in LA preparing for the role, Jonah was invited to dinner by Chris and Emma to meet with Guy. 'Guy shows up, and I'm a bit nervous, because he's a movie star and he's doing the film. So I try to be cool, and I notice that creeping out from underneath one of the sleeves from his T-shirt down his arm was a tattoo – the one on his left bicep. They had been testing the tattoos that day, to make sure they would look right. It suddenly dawned on me that this was the first time I'd ever seen something that resembled my work published. It was a very surreal moment.'

An extreme form of publication, it seems appropriate that Jonah's words should first be displayed to the world on someone's flesh, resembling Leonard's own method of recording his story. His debut over, Jonah turned to the matter in hand: the ending. It was clear to all that the audience needed a resolution, at least with the John G. character, who never makes an appearance in the film, other than as a masked man, in the briefest glimpse of a shot.

> The original idea was – and this had come directly from my experience in Madrid – that the person who had committed the crime, violent anonymous crime, was going to remain anonymous. They may as well cease to exist because you're never going to find them. How would I find three guys who mugged me in Madrid three years ago? They vanish. Leonard cannot find John G. He won't get the satisfaction of finding the guy and killing him; but it was pointed out that it may be too much for the audience – to come through this whole journey and find nothing. We came up with this idea that perhaps Leonard had already found him, and he was dead.

While less ambiguous than initially intended, it actually leaves the viewer with far more to think on. Leonard is no longer the lone avenger but a serial murderer with a severe case of denial. Add the fact that Nolan has already, for the observant ones amongst us, led us to speculate on whether Leonard spent a period of time in a mental institution (his face fractionally replacing that of Sammy's in the scene where Jankis is admitted) and the final flourish is a piece of bravura film-making. An extended sequence that knits together the forwards-objective black-and-white strand with the backwards-subjective colour sequence, the film loops back on itself as Leonard's Polaroid of Jimmy's corpse develops, fading us into glorious Technicolor. As the sequence heads to join up with the moment where Leonard screeches to a halt outside of Emma's tattoo parlour (providing one almighty jolt as the film concludes), a multitude of ideas comes into play. With the revelation that Leonard may already have killed the true assailant but forgotten the action, we witness the beginning to another cycle of detection and destruction for the protagonist. Condemned by his foolhardy revelation that he too is a John G., Teddy becomes the next target for Leonard, as he slips down that ever-widening gyre.

'It is a film without a beginning,' says Nolan. 'In terms of the story, because it's told in reverse, the story is this backwards spiral, an implosion. When you step back from that, and view it chronologically, objectively, you realize it's an explosion. The more tightly you wrap up the end, the more you exaggerate the explosion. It was a nice irony – the more answers you tried to provide, the more ambiguities you would raise.'

Think of the file Leonard carries with him, missing pages and with sections crossed out. Whether Leonard vandalized the file himself or not, it becomes the perfect symbol for the film. All the answers, one would imagine, are contained in there, but obscured. As we progress, we learn how Leonard obtained the conclusive fact – Teddy's licence-plate number – that puts him on the trail; we also see when the oft-obeyed 'Don't Believe His Lies' was written on the Polaroid of Teddy. By now, with Leonard confessing the fact that he is capable of lying to himself to be happy, we begin to think that it is Leonard's words we should not trust. With the brief shot of Leonard in bed with his wife, with 'I've Done It' inscribed on the bare patch of flesh over his heart, perhaps Leonard did once have such a tattoo; perhaps his wife, who survived the rape, suggested it, hoping her husband would remember the actions he undertook with Teddy; perhaps Leonard did cause her insulin overdose, and was admitted to a mental asylum, then later escaped. Or perhaps it's just a fantasy. Perhaps Leonard, as Jennifer Todd thinks, is telling the truth:

> I don't think Leonard did kill his wife, though the website makes you think he did. I think Teddy is lying to him at the end. There was a Sammy Jankis, and Leonard did get the same condition. Emma agreed with me – at least that night [at the Venice Film festival].

People ask me about the ending, and more women want to believe that Leonard didn't kill his wife than men do. I also think mine is the more literal version. I'm the simple person who wants to believe what we've seen.

Seeing, indeed, may be believing, but eyes can deceive. Nolan argues that by the ending we have become distrustful of the mental images shown, to the point that we no longer are willing to accept Leonard's account of the rape. That said, the confessional telephone conversations Leonard has in the black-and-white sequences potentially seem to ring true. Early on, we are verbally warned as to how Leonard will be treated. 'You have to be wary of other people writing stuff for you that's not going to make sense, or will lead you astray. I dunno. I guess people try and take advantage of somebody with this condition.' Towards the end of the film, Nolan again draws parallels between the lives of Sammy and Leonard, who says: 'You know the truth about my condition, officer? You don't know anything. You feel angry, you don't know why. You feel guilty, you have no idea why. You could do anything, and not have the faintest idea ten minutes later. Like Sammy. What if I'd done something like Sammy?'

The split, as Nolan sees it, between those who believe Leonard didn't kill his wife and those who think he did comes from the difference between visual and verbal memory. 'If you believe what you've seen in the film, you come to one conclusion. If you believe what you've heard, you come to another. That wasn't something I thought about when I was doing it, but it arises naturally from the situation, the expositional scene. What I'm finding is that most people are very reluctant to abandon the idea of their visual memory. People believe their eyes more than their ears.' If, by now, you are still seeking the answer to the riddle that is *Memento*, it's sound advice.

Appendix

Memento Mori
A short story by Jonathan Nolan

'What like a bullet can undeceive!'
Herman Melville

*Your wife always used to say you'd be late for your own funeral.
Remember that? Her little joke because you were such a slob – always
late, always forgetting stuff, even before the incident.*

Right about now you're probably wondering if you were late for hers.

*You were there, you can be sure of that. That's what the picture's for
– the one tacked to the wall by the door. It's not customary to take pictures
at a funeral, but somebody, your doctors, I guess, knew you wouldn't
remember. They had it blown up nice and big and stuck it right there,
next to the door, so you couldn't help but see it every time you got up
to find out where she was.*

*The guy in the picture, the one with the flowers? That's you. And
what are you doing? You're reading the headstone, trying to figure out
whose funeral you're at, same as you're reading it now, trying to figure
why someone stuck that picture next to your door. But why bother
reading something that you won't remember?*

*She's gone, gone for good, and you must be hurting right now, hearing
the news. Believe me, I know how you feel. You're probably a wreck.
But give it five minutes, maybe ten. Maybe you can even go a whole
half-hour before you forget.*

*But you will forget – I guarantee it. A few more minutes and you'll
be heading for the door, looking for her all over again, breaking down
when you find the picture. How many times do you have to hear the
news before some other part of your body, other than that busted brain
of yours, starts to remember?*

*Never-ending grief, never-ending anger. Useless without direction.
Maybe you can't understand what's happened. Can't say I really
understand, either. Backwards amnesia. That's what the sign says.
CRS disease. Your guess is as good as mine.*

Maybe you can't understand what happened to you. But you do remember what happened to HER, don't you? The doctors don't want to talk about it. They won't answer my questions. They don't think it's right for a man in your condition to hear about those things. But you remember enough, don't you? You remember his face.

This is why I'm writing to you. Futile, maybe. I don't know how many times you'll have to read this before you listen to me. I don't even know how long you've been locked up in this room already. Neither do you. But your advantage in forgetting is that you'll forget to write yourself off as a lost cause.

Sooner or later you'll want to do something about it. And when you do, you'll just have to trust me, because I'm the only one who can help you.

EARL OPENS ONE EYE after another to a stretch of white ceiling tiles interrupted by a hand-printed sign taped right above his head, large enough for him to read from the bed. An alarm clock is ringing somewhere. He reads the sign, blinks, reads it again, then takes a look at the room.

It's a white room, overwhelmingly white, from the walls and the curtains to the institutional furniture and the bedspread.

The alarm clock is ringing from the white desk under the window with the white curtains. At this point Earl probably notices that he is lying on top of his white comforter. He is already wearing a dressing gown and slippers.

He lies back and reads the sign taped to the ceiling again. It says, in crude block capitals, THIS IS YOUR ROOM. THIS IS A ROOM IN A HOSPITAL. THIS IS WHERE YOU LIVE NOW.

Earl rises and takes a look around. The room is large for a hospital – empty linoleum stretches out from the bed in three directions. Two doors and a window. The view isn't very helpful, either – a close of trees in the centre of a carefully manicured piece of turf that terminates in a sliver of two-lane blacktop. The trees, except for the evergreens, are bare – early spring or late fall, one or the other.

Every inch of the desk is covered with Post-it notes, legal pads, neatly printed lists, psychological textbooks, framed pictures. On top of the mess is a half-completed crossword puzzle. The alarm clock is riding a pile of folded newspapers. Earl slaps the snooze button and takes a cigarette from the pack taped to the sleeve of his dressing gown. He pats the empty pockets of his pyjamas for a light. He rifles the papers on the desk, looks quickly through the drawers. Eventually he finds a box of kitchen matches taped to the wall next to the window. Another sign is taped just above the box. It says in loud yellow letters, CIGARETTE? CHECK FOR LIT ONES FIRST, STUPID.

Earl laughs at the sign, lights his cigarette, and takes a long draw. Taped to the window in front of him is another piece of loose-leaf paper headed YOUR SCHEDULE.

It charts off the hours, every hour, in blocks: 10:00 p.m. to 8:00 a.m. is labelled GO BACK TO SLEEP. Earl consults the alarm clock: 8:15. Given the light outside, it must be morning. He checks his watch: 10:30. He presses the watch to his ear and listens. He gives the watch a wind or two and sets it to match the alarm clock.

According to the schedule, the entire block from 8:00 to 8:30 has been labelled brush your teeth. Earl laughs again and walks over to the bathroom.

The bathroom window is open. As he flaps his arms to keep warm, he notices the ashtray on the window sill. A cigarette is perched on the ashtray, burning steadily through a long finger of ash. He frowns, extinguishes the old butt, and replaces it with the new one.

The toothbrush has already been treated to a smudge of white paste. The tap is of the push-button variety – a dose of water with each nudge. Earl pushes the brush into his cheek and fiddles it back and forth while he opens the medicine cabinet. The shelves are stocked with single-serving packages of vitamins, aspirin, anti-diuretics. The mouthwash is also single-serving, about a shot-glass-worth of blue liquid in a sealed plastic bottle. Only the toothpaste is regular-sized. Earl spits the paste out of his mouth and replaces it with the mouthwash. As he lays the toothbrush next to the toothpaste, he notices a tiny wedge of paper pinched between the glass shelf and the steel backing of the medicine cabinet. He spits the frothy blue fluid into the sink and nudges for some more water to rinse it down. He closes the medicine cabinet and smiles at his reflection in the mirror.

'Who needs half an hour to brush their teeth?'

The paper has been folded down to a minuscule size with all the precision of a sixth-grader's love note. Earl unfolds it and smoothes it against the mirror. It reads –

IF YOU CAN STILL READ THIS, THEN YOU'RE A FUCKING COWARD.

Earl stares blankly at the paper, then reads it again. He turns it over.

On the back it reads –
P.S.: AFTER YOU'VE READ THIS HIDE IT AGAIN.
Earl reads both sides again, then folds the note back down to its original size and tucks it underneath the toothpaste.

Maybe then he notices the scar. It begins just beneath the ear, jagged and thick, and disappears abruptly into his hairline. Earl turns his head and stares out of the corner of his eye to follow the scar's progress. He traces it with a fingertip, then looks back down at the cigarette burning in the ashtray. A thought seizes him and he spins out of the bathroom.

He is caught at the door to his room, one hand on the knob. Two pictures are taped to the wall by the door. Earl's attention is caught first by the MRI, a shiny black frame for four windows into someone's skull. In marker, the picture is labelled YOUR BRAIN. Earl stares at it. Concentric circles in different colours. He can make out the big orbs of his eyes and, behind these, the twin lobes of his brain. Smooth wrinkles, circles, semi-circles. But right there in the middle of his head, circled in marker, tunnelled in from the back of his neck like a maggot into an apricot, is something different. Deformed, broken, but unmistakable. A dark smudge, the shape of a flower, right there in the middle of his brain.

He bends to look at the other picture. It is a photograph of a man holding flowers, standing over a fresh grave. The man is bent over, reading the headstone. For a moment this looks like a hall of mirrors or the beginnings of a sketch of infinity: the one man bent over, looking at the smaller man, bent over, reading the headstone. Earl looks at the picture for a long time. Maybe he begins to cry. Maybe he just stares silently at the picture. Eventually, he makes his way back to the bed, flops down, seals his eyes shut, tries to sleep.

The cigarette burns steadily away in the bathroom. A circuit in the alarm clock counts down from ten, and it starts ringing again.

Earl opens one eye after another to a stretch of white ceiling tiles, interrupted by a hand-printed sign taped right above his head, large enough for him to read from the bed.

You can't have a normal life anymore. You must know that. How can you have a girlfriend if you can't remember her name? Can't have kids, not unless you want them to grow up with a dad who doesn't recognize them. Sure as hell can't hold down a job. Not too many professions out there that value forgetfulness. Prostitution, maybe. Politics, of course. No. Your life is over. You're a dead man. The only thing the doctors are hoping to do is teach you to be less of a burden to the orderlies. And they'll probably never let you go home, wherever that would be.

So the question is not 'to be or not to be,' because you aren't. The question is whether you want to do something about it. Whether revenge matters to you.

It does to most people. For a few weeks, they plot, they scheme, they take measures to get even. But the passage of time is all it takes to erode that initial impulse. Time is theft, isn't that what they say? And time eventually convinces most of us that forgiveness is a virtue. Conveniently, cowardice and forgiveness look identical at a certain distance. Time steals your nerve.

If time and fear aren't enough to dissuade people from their revenge, then there's always authority, softly shaking its head and saying, We understand, but you're the better man for letting it go. For rising above it. For not sinking to their level. And besides, says authority, if you try anything stupid, we'll lock you up in a little room.

But they already put you in a little room, didn't they? Only they don't really lock it or even guard it too carefully because you're a cripple. A corpse. A vegetable who probably wouldn't remember to eat or take a shit if someone wasn't there to remind you.

And as for the passage of time, well, that doesn't really apply to you anymore, does it? Just the same ten minutes, over and over again. So how can you forgive if you can't remember to forget?

You probably were the type to let it go, weren't you? Before.

But you're not the man you used to be. Not even half. You're a fraction; you're the ten-minute man.

Of course, weakness is strong. It's the primary impulse. You'd probably prefer to sit in your little room and cry. Live in your finite collection of memories, carefully polishing each one. Half a life set behind glass and pinned to cardboard like a collection of exotic insects. You'd like to live behind that glass, wouldn't you? Preserved in aspic.

You'd like to but you can't, can you? You can't because of the last addition to your collection. The last thing you remember. His face. His face and your wife, looking to you for help.

And maybe this is where you can retire to when it's over. Your little collection. They can lock you back up in another little room and you can live the rest of your life in the past. But only if you've got a little piece of paper in your hand that says you got him.

You know I'm right. You know there's a lot of work to do. It may seem impossible, but I'm sure if we all do our part, we'll figure something out. But you don't have much time. You've only got about ten minutes, in fact. Then it starts all over again. So do something with the time you've got.

EARL OPENS HIS EYES and blinks into the darkness. The alarm clock is ringing. It says 3:20, and the moonlight streaming through the window means it must be the early morning. Earl fumbles for the lamp, almost knocking it over in the process. Incandescent light fills the room, painting the metal furniture yellow, the walls yellow, the bedspread, too. He lies back and looks up at the stretch of yellow ceiling tiles above him, interrupted by a handwritten sign taped to the ceiling. He reads the sign two, maybe three times, then blinks at the room around him.

It is a bare room. Institutional, maybe. There is a desk over by the window. The desk is bare except for the blaring alarm clock. Earl probably notices, at this point, that he is fully clothed. He even has his shoes on under the sheets. He extracts himself from the bed and crosses to the desk. Nothing in the room would suggest that anyone lived there, or ever had, except for the odd scrap of tape stuck here and there to the wall. No pictures, no books, nothing. Through the window, he can see a full moon shining on carefully manicured grass.

Earl slaps the snooze button on the alarm clock and stares a moment at the two keys taped to the back of his hand. He picks at the tape while he searches through the empty drawers. In the left pocket of his jacket, he finds a roll of hundred-dollar bills and a letter sealed in an envelope. He checks the rest of the main room and the bathroom. Bits of tape, cigarette butts. Nothing else.

Earl absentmindedly plays with the lump of scar tissue on his neck and moves back toward the bed. He lies back down and stares up at the ceiling and the sign taped to it. The sign reads, GET UP, GET OUT RIGHT NOW. THESE PEOPLE ARE TRYING TO KILL YOU.

Earl closes his eyes.

They tried to teach you to make lists in grade school, remember? Back when your day planner was the back of your hand. And if your assignments came off in the shower, well, then they didn't get done.

No direction, they said. No discipline. So they tried to get you to write it all down somewhere more permanent.

Of course, your grade-school teachers would be laughing their pants wet if they could see you now. Because you've become the exact product of their organizational lessons. Because you can't even take a piss without consulting one of your lists.

They were right. Lists are the only way out of this mess.

Here's the truth: People, even regular people, are never just any one person with one set of attributes. It's not that simple. We're all at the mercy of the limbic system, clouds of electricity drifting through the brain. Every man is broken into twenty-four-hour fractions, and then again within those twenty-four hours. It's a daily pantomime, one man yielding control to the next: a backstage crowded with old hacks clamouring for their turn in the spotlight. Every week, every day. The angry man hands the baton over to the sulking man, and in turn to the sex addict, the introvert, the conversationalist. Every man is a mob, a chain gang of idiots.

This is the tragedy of life. Because for a few minutes of every day, every man becomes a genius. Moments of clarity, insight, whatever you want to call them. The clouds part, the planets get in a neat little line, and everything becomes obvious. I should quit smoking, maybe, or here's how I could make a fast million, or such and such is the key to eternal happiness. That's the miserable truth. For a few moments, the secrets of the universe are opened to us. Life is a cheap parlour trick.

But then the genius, the savant, has to hand over the controls to the next guy down the pike, most likely the guy who just wants to eat potato chips, and insight and brilliance and salvation are all entrusted to a moron or a hedonist or a narcoleptic.

The only way out of this mess, of course, is to take steps to ensure that you control the idiots that you become. To take your chain gang, hand in hand, and lead them. The best way to do this is with a list.

It's like a letter you write to yourself. A master plan, drafted by the guy who can see the light, made with steps simple enough for the rest of the idiots to understand. Follow steps one through one hundred. Repeat as necessary.

Your problem is a little more acute, maybe, but fundamentally the same thing.

It's like that computer thing, the Chinese room. You remember that? One guy sits in a little room, laying down cards with letters written on *them in a language he doesn't understand, laying them down one letter at a time in a sequence according to someone else's instructions. The cards are supposed to spell out a joke in Chinese. The guy doesn't speak Chinese, of course. He just follows his instructions.*

There are some obvious differences in your situation, of course: You broke out of the room they had you in, so the whole enterprise has to be portable. And the guy giving the instructions – that's you, too, just an earlier version of you. And the joke you're telling, well, it's got a punch line. I just don't think anyone's going to find it very funny.

So that's the idea. All you have to do is follow your instructions. Like climbing a ladder or descending a staircase. One step at a time. Right down the list. Simple.

And the secret, of course, to any list is to keep it in a place where you're bound to see it.

HE CAN HEAR THE BUZZING through his eyelids. Insistent. He reaches out for the alarm clock, but he can't move his arm.

Earl opens his eyes to see a large man bent double over him. The man looks up at him, annoyed, then resumes his work. Earl looks around him. Too dark for a doctor's office.

Then the pain floods his brain, blocking out the other questions. He squirms again, trying to yank his forearm away, the one that feels like it's burning. The arm doesn't move, but the man shoots him another scowl. Earl adjusts himself in the chair to see over the top of the man's head.

The noise and the pain are both coming from a gun in the man's hand – a gun with a needle where the barrel should be. The needle is digging into the fleshy underside of Earl's forearm, leaving a trail of puffy letters behind it.

Earl tries to rearrange himself to get a better view, to read the letters on his arm, but he can't. He lies back and stares at the ceiling.

Eventually the tattoo artist turns off the noise, wipes Earl's forearm with a piece of gauze, and wanders over to the back to dig up a pamphlet describing how to deal with a possible infection. Maybe later he'll tell his wife about this guy and his little note. Maybe his wife will convince him to call the police.

Earl looks down at the arm. The letters are rising up from the skin, weeping a little. They run from just behind the strap of Earl's watch all the way to the inside of his elbow. Earl blinks at the message and reads it again. It says, in careful little capitals, I RAPED AND KILLED YOUR WIFE.

It's your birthday today, so I got you a little present. I would have just bought you a beer, but who knows where that would have ended?

So instead, I got you a bell. I think I may have had to pawn your watch to buy it, but what the hell did you need a watch for, anyway?

You're probably asking yourself, Why a bell? In fact, I'm guessing you're going to be asking yourself that question every time you find it in your pocket. Too many of these letters now. Too many for you to dig back into every time you want to know the answer to some little question.

It's a joke, actually. A practical joke. But think of it this way: I'm not really laughing at you so much as with you.

I'd like to think that every time you take it out of your pocket and wonder, Why do I have this bell? a little part of you, a little piece of your broken brain, will remember and laugh, like I'm laughing now.

Besides, you do know the answer. It was something you learned before. So if you think about it, you'll know.

Back in the old days, people were obsessed with the fear of being buried alive. You remember now? Medical science not being quite what it is today, it wasn't uncommon for people to suddenly wake up in a casket.

So rich folks had their coffins outfitted with breathing tubes. Little tubes running up to the mud above so that if someone woke up when they weren't supposed to, they wouldn't run out of oxygen. Now, they must have tested this out and realized that you could shout yourself hoarse through the tube, but it was too narrow to carry much noise. Not enough to attract attention, at least. So a string was run up the tube to a little bell attached to the headstone. If a dead person came back to life, all he had to do was ring his little bell till someone came and dug him up again.

I'm laughing now, picturing you on a bus or maybe in a fast-food restaurant, reaching into your pocket and finding your little bell and wondering to yourself where it came from, why you have it. Maybe you'll even ring it.

Happy birthday, buddy.

I don't know who figured out the solution to our mutual problem, so I don't know whether to congratulate you or me. A bit of a lifestyle change, admittedly, but an elegant solution, nonetheless.

191

Look to yourself for the answer.

That sounds like something out of a Hallmark card. I don't know when you thought it up, but my hat's off to you. Not that you know what the hell I'm talking about. But, honestly, a real brainstorm. After all, everybody else needs mirrors to remind themselves who they are. You're no different.

THE LITTLE MECHANICAL VOICE PAUSES, then repeats itself. It says, 'The time is 8:00 a.m. This is a courtesy call.' Earl opens his eyes and replaces the receiver. The phone is perched on a cheap veneer headboard that stretches behind the bed, curves to meet the corner, and ends at the mini-bar. The TV is still on, blobs of flesh colour nattering away at each other. Earl lies back down and is surprised to see himself, older now, tanned, the hair pulling away from his head like solar flares. The mirror on the ceiling is cracked, the silver fading in creases. Earl continues to stare at himself, astonished by what he sees. He is fully dressed, but the clothes are old, threadbare in places.

Earl feels the familiar spot on his left wrist for his watch, but it's gone. He looks down from the mirror to his arm. It is bare and the skin has changed to an even tan, as if he never owned a watch in the first place. The skin is even in colour except for the solid black arrow on the inside of Earl's wrist, pointing up his shirtsleeve. He stares at the arrow for a moment. Perhaps he doesn't try to rub it off anymore. He rolls up his sleeve.

The arrow points to a sentence tattooed along Earl's inner arm. Earl reads the sentence once, maybe twice. Another arrow picks up at the beginning of the sentence, points farther up Earl's arm, disappearing under the rolled-up shirtsleeve. He unbuttons his shirt.

Looking down on his chest, he can make out the shapes but cannot bring them into focus, so he looks up at the mirror above him.

The arrow leads up Earl's arm, crosses at the shoulder, and descends on to his upper torso, terminating at a picture of a man's face that occupies most of his chest. The face is that of a large man, balding, with a moustache and a goatee. It is a particular face, but like a police sketch it has a certain unreal quality.

The rest of his upper torso is covered in words, phrases, bits of information, and instructions, all of them written backward on Earl, forward in the mirror.

Eventually Earl sits up, buttons his shirt, and crosses to the desk. He takes out a pen and a piece of notepaper from the desk drawer, sits, and begins to write.

I don't know where you'll be when you read this. I'm not even sure if you'll bother to read this. I guess you don't need to.

It's a shame, really, that you and I will never meet. But, like the song says, 'By the time you read this note, I'll be gone.'

We're so close now. That's the way it feels. So many pieces put together, spelled out. I guess it's just a matter of time until you find him.

Who knows what we've done to get here? Must be a hell of a story, if only you could remember any of it. I guess it's better that you can't.

I had a thought just now. Maybe you'll find it useful.

Everybody is waiting for the end to come, but what if it already passed us by? What if the final joke of Judgement Day was that it had already come and gone and we were none the wiser? Apocalypse arrives quietly; the chosen are herded off to heaven, and the rest of us, the ones who failed the test, just keep on going, oblivious. Dead already, wandering around long after the gods have stopped keeping score, still optimistic about the future.

I guess if that's true, then it doesn't matter what you do. No expectations. If you can't find him, then it doesn't matter, because nothing matters. And if you do find him, then you can kill him without worrying about the consequences. Because there are no consequences.

That's what I'm thinking about right now, in this scrappy little room. Framed pictures of ships on the wall. I don't know, obviously, but if I had to guess, I'd say we're somewhere up the coast. If you're wondering why your left arm is five shades browner than your right, I don't know what to tell you. I guess we must have been driving for a while. And, no, I don't know what happened to your watch.

And all these keys: I have no idea. Not a one that I recognize. Car keys and house keys and the little fiddly keys for padlocks. What have we been up to?

I wonder if he'll feel stupid when you find him. Tracked down by the ten-minute man. Assassinated by a vegetable.

I'll be gone in a moment. I'll put down the pen, close my eyes, and then you can read this through if you want.

I just wanted you to know that I'm proud of you. No one who matters is left to say it. No one left is going to want to.

EARL'S EYES ARE WIDE OPEN, staring through the window of the car. Smiling eyes. Smiling through the window at the crowd gathering across the street. The crowd gathering around the body in the doorway. The body emptying slowly across the sidewalk and into the storm drain.

A stocky guy, face down, eyes open. Balding head, goatee. In death, as in police sketches, faces tend to look the same. This is definitely somebody in particular. But really, it could be anybody.

Earl is still smiling at the body as the car pulls away from the curb. The car? Who's to say? Maybe it's a police cruiser. Maybe it's just a taxi.

As the car is swallowed into traffic, Earl's eyes continue to shine out into the night, watching the body until it disappears into a circle of concerned pedestrians. He chuckles to himself as the car continues to make distance between him and the growing crowd.

Earl's smile fades a little. Something has occurred to him. He begins to pat down his pockets; leisurely at first, like a man looking for his keys, then a little more desperately. Maybe his progress is impeded by a set of handcuffs. He begins to empty the contents of his pockets out on to the seat next to him. Some money. A bunch of keys. Scraps of paper.

A round metal lump rolls out of his pocket and slides across the vinyl seat. Earl is frantic now. He hammers at the plastic divider between him and the driver, begging the man for a pen. Perhaps the cabbie doesn't speak much English. Perhaps the cop isn't in the habit of talking to suspects. Either way, the divider between the man in front and the man behind remains closed. A pen is not forthcoming.

The car hits a pothole, and Earl blinks at his reflection in the rearview mirror. He is calm now. The driver makes another corner, and the metal lump slides back over to rest against Earl's leg with a little jingle. He picks it up and looks at it, curious now. It is a little bell. A little metal bell. Inscribed on it are his name and a set of dates. He recognizes the first one: the year in which he was born. But the second date means nothing to him. Nothing at all.

As he turns the bell over in his hands, he notices the empty space on his wrist where his watch used to sit. There is a little arrow there, pointing up his arm. Earl looks at the arrow, then begins to roll up his sleeve. 'You'd be late for your own funeral,' she'd say. Remember? The more I think about it, the more trite that seems. What kind of idiot, after all, is in any kind of rush to get to the end of his own story?

And how would I know if I were late, anyway? I don't have a watch anymore. I don't know what we did with it.

What the hell do you need a watch for, anyway? It was an antique. Deadweight tugging at your wrist. Symbol of the old you. The you that believed in time.

No. Scratch that. It's not so much that you've lost your faith in time as that time has lost its faith in you. And who needs it, anyway? Who wants to be one of those saps living in the safety of the future, in the safety of the moment after the moment in which they felt something powerful? Living in the next moment, in which they feel nothing. Crawling down the hands of the clock, away from the people who did unspeakable things to them. Believing the lie that time will heal all wounds – which is just a nice way of saying that time deadens us.

But you're different. You're more perfect. Time is three things for most people, but for you, for us, just one. A singularity. One moment. This moment. Like you're the centre of the clock, the axis on which the hands turn. Time moves about you but never moves you. It has lost its ability to affect you. What is it they say? That time is theft? But not for you. Close your eyes and you can start all over again. Conjure up that necessary emotion, fresh as roses.

Time is an absurdity. An abstraction. The only thing that matters is this moment. This moment a million times over. You have to trust me. If this moment is repeated enough, if you keep trying – and you have to keep trying – eventually you will come across the next item on your list.